GEOFF HILL writes a popular column the author of *Way to Go: Two of th Journeys, The Road To Gobblers Knob. Motorbike* and *Anyway, Where Was I? Geoff Hill's Alternative A to Z of the World.* He has either won or been shortlisted for a UK Travel Writer of the Year award nine times and is a former European Travel Writer of the Year. He has written about travel for the *Irish Times, Daily Telegraph* and the *Independent on Sunday.*

COLIN O'CARROLL was born in Belfast in 1962. He emigrated to Australia at the age of ten, where he developed a passion for motorcycling and began a career as a journalist. He returned to live in his native city in the early nineties and took on a variety of journalistic roles, including that of roving reporter with Downtown Radio and editor of *Daily Ireland.* He has also written for the *Irish News, Irish Independent* and *Daily Mirror.* He is currently deputy news editor with the *Belfast Telegraph.*

around Australia
on a Triumph

GEOFF HILL
& COLIN O'CARROLL

BLACKSTAFF
PRESS

BELFAST

First published in 2010 by
Blackstaff Press
4c Heron Wharf, Sydenham Business Park
Belfast, BT3 9LE
with the assistance of
The Arts Council of Northern Ireland

arts
council
of Northern Ireland

Typeset by CJWT Solutions, St Helens

Printed in Great Britain by the MPG Books Group

A CIP catalogue record for this book is available from the British Library

ISBN 978-0-85640-857-1

www.blackstaffpress.com

Our thanks to Cate and Catherine, our respective better halves, for letting us bugger off for three months.
And for letting us come back again.

The first question which you will ask and which I must try to answer is this, 'What is the use of climbing Mount Everest?' and my answer must at once be, It is no use. There is not the slightest prospect of any gain whatsoever. Oh, we may learn a little about the behaviour of the human body at high altitudes, and possibly medical men may turn our observation to some account for the purposes of aviation. But otherwise nothing will come of it. We shall not bring back a single bit of gold or silver, not a gem, nor any coal or iron. We shall not find a single foot of earth that can be planted with crops to raise food. It's no use. So, if you cannot understand that there is something in man which responds to the challenge of this mountain and goes out to meet it, that the struggle is the struggle of life itself upward and forever upward, then you won't see why we go.

What we get from this adventure is just sheer joy. And joy is, after all, the end of life. We do not live to eat and make money. We eat and make money to be able to enjoy life. That is what life means and what life is for.

GEORGE MALLORY, 1922

(Yes, we know he later died climbing Everest, but that's not the point)

Geoff Hill

 Colin O'Carroll

David Gulpilil, Lucien John and Jenny Agutter in *Walkabout* (1971)

I

I knew everything there was to know about Australia. After watching *Crocodile Dundee* and *Priscilla, Queen of the Desert*, I knew that men wrestled crocodiles, shaved with knives and dressed up as women. From further research at the local video store, I also knew that schoolgirls shouldn't have picnics at hanging rocks, and that at any given moment you were likely to round a corner and find Jenny Agutter swimming naked in a billabong. Whatever a billabong was.

Australia was an elemental land where all the men were called Bruce, and all the women Sheila.

For an Australian bloke, the most important things in life were your mates, drinking beer, and drinking beer with your mates, and the worst thing you could be was a Pom or a poofta. Poms were easy to recognise because they couldn't play cricket, and pooftas because they didn't like footie and they understood sheilas. The only exception to this was Clive James, who wasn't a poofta, but had become a Pom by osmosis. If a bloke did turn out to be a poofta, the only way out was to dress up as a sheila and drive a bus called Priscilla across the outback.

As for sheilas, their job was to keep their blokes happy and have a hot steak and a cold beer ready at the right time, usually three in the morning when their blokes came home from the pub. If a sheila was stupid enough to get herself pregnant, her only recourse was to throw herself off Sydney Harbour Bridge, plummeting towards the waiting sharks in a floral chiffon frock with Bruce's parting words ringing in her ears: 'You're pregnant and you're going to kill yourself? Jesus, Sheila, you're a sport!'

Yes, I could safely say I knew everything there was to know about Australia. Until I met Colin, and everything changed.

Originally from Belfast, my family had moved to Australia in 1972 after the onset of the Troubles. They had hung on for a couple of years but, correctly judging that this was one show that would run and run and knowing that they didn't want to sit through to the finale, decided to emigrate 'Down Under'. At that time, the Australian government was running the 'Ten Pound Tourists' scheme, an assisted passage incentive that had been introduced to the United Kingdom following the Second World War and which had been particularly popular in Northern Ireland during the sixties and seventies. As a kid, I was torn between the excitement of moving to the land of Skippy, koalas and surfing, and the misery of leaving all my relatives and friends behind. But it was all academic anyway, as I had no real choice in the matter and so we found ourselves packing up for a whole new life.

It took us six weeks to travel there, as we went by ship, and when we arrived we made our home in Melbourne, in the state of Victoria. It took a while to settle in as there were a lot of bitey nasties lurking about, but once they realised they couldn't hold out against a bunch of war-hardened Belfast urchins and scarpered, we managed to relax and enjoy the blistering heat.

I loved growing up in Australia. I learned how to surf and how to ride a motorbike and, when I decided to begin a career in journalism, it was in Australia that I got my first job. After several stints working in Oz, Asia and assorted other news hotspots around the world, curiosity and the promise of work covering the Troubles brought me back to Belfast at the age of thirty. For the next seventeen years I had what can only be described as a varied career, working for various Northern Irish newspapers and broadcasters.

Now, I'm in the unusual yet enviable position of having two places to call home, Belfast and Melbourne, but also in the unenviable position of always being homesick in one or the other.

 Colin had spent his youth snogging sharks, wrestling kangaroos and riding dirt bikes through the outback, before coming back to Belfast for a bit of peace and quiet. In the middle of the Troubles. Eventually he ended up working on the same paper as me.

'Pies, mate,' he said one evening when I mentioned the subject of Australia, polishing off the last of his beer, crushing the tin and tossing it in a familiar arc onto the growing pile in the bin.

'Pies?' I said, in the manner of a man unused to such Antipodean succinctness, having been brought up on the extravagant peregrinations of such icons of Irish literature as Flann O'Brien, a writer who had infused in me the sure and certain knowledge that when it came to language, the worst thing you could do was to cut a long story short.

'Pies,' said Colin, popping another tinny open with a masterly air. 'Your Australian pie is the biggest danger you can face Down Under.'

'And why,' I said hesitantly, opening a beer myself with the feeling that if I could not beat him, I may as well join him, 'is that?'

'Well, your Australian meat pie can be tepid on the outside, lulling you into a false sense of security, so that you bite into it only to discover that the centre is the temperature of a nuclear reactor. Many's the time I've been at a cricket match when the lull between overs is interrupted by a blood-curdling scream, in the gurgling aftermath of which neighbours will turn to each other and say, "Pie?" then nod knowingly and open another stubby.'

'Good grief,' I said, my dreams of a naked Jenny Agutter sinking into the murky silt at the bottom of my consciousness.

'And then, of course, there's your bull ant. Two inches long, and half of that's jaw. I remember riding my bike once down by the beach, and putting my foot down for a second. The next thing I knew, I'd thrown the bike down and was sprinting through the bush tearing my daks off and trying to get three of the bastards out of my thigh. Threw myself in the water to drown them, and the next thing I knew a bloody great tiger shark comes swimming by. Course, the sharks are always cruising by down there looking for pooftas who use body boards rather than proper surfboards. "Shark biscuits", we call them, cos that's what they look like to a shark.'

'Aren't there any cuddly things in Australia?' I said helplessly. 'Like wombats?'

'Wombats? Bloody speed bumps. They have this hard ridge of cartilage along their backs so that the dingos can't get them when they bury themselves in their burrows for the night. And they go to sleep in the middle of the road at night because it's warm. Hit them on a bike at seventy and you go sailing off into the night, while the bloody wombat picks itself up, dusts itself off and trundles off for a nice tasty eucalyptus supper.'

'Or a pie,' I said glumly, my vision of the last cuddly animal in Australia going the same way as Jenny Agutter.

'Listen,' said Colin, coming back from the fridge with two more beers, 'the only way you're going to find out is to go there. Why don't we rustle up a couple of bikes and ride all the way around Oz on Highway One? It's only 15,000 miles or so.' He paused. 'And besides, it's about time you learned to do a wheelie.'

He was right. Wheelies, like stoppies, doughnuts and getting my knee down on corners, had eluded me through my short but eventful motorcycle life. You see, I may have ridden a Royal Enfield from Delhi to Belfast, a Harley from Chicago to

Los Angeles and a Triumph from Chile to Alaska, but in the depths of my heart there lurked the suspicion that I was a bluffer rather than a proper biker.

I, on the other hand, had been a motorbike nut since early childhood when, at the tender age of eleven, I got my first bike. It was a home-made minibike, made out of welded steel, wheelbarrow wheels and a lawnmower engine. It had no gears, no brakes and to start it you had to run like buggery and jump on. If it didn't go, you did it again until you were exhausted. If the motor did catch, you hung on for dear life, and could only dismount when you ran out of petrol. That or aim for something soft and bale out. It was the start of a passion that would last all my life.

I soon progressed to bigger, faster machines, started racing motocross and other types of competition, and broke bones at a rate that would have had Evel Knievel in a cold sweat. On top of that, being a journo has allowed me to indulge in my passion in various other ways over the years, from covering stories on bikes to blagging my way into Grands Prix and various other events all over the world.

Continuing to ride bikes as a hobby, even in the depths of the dark, cold, wet and sometimes freezing Irish winters, helped me retain my credibility as a serious biker – even if sometimes I secretly wished I'd been born with a penchant for leather-upholstered, heated stretch limos, rather than oil-sodden leathers – so it wouldn't take much to convince me to go on any two-wheeled adventure.

I'd always wanted to do another long trip in Australia ever since, aged just seventeen, I failed to cross the continent from south to north through the Red Centre on my little 125cc two-stroke scrambler. The bike broke down around 800 miles or so south of Alice Springs and I'd had to abandon it, managing to get a lift with one of my high-school teachers of all people, who just happened to be passing by in his Land Rover on his own summer holiday adventure.

It was probably just as well I failed as I was woefully ill-equipped for a desert crossing – the bike was underpowered, I couldn't carry enough water or supplies and I was travelling through the heat of summer. The desert is littered with the skeletons of people just as foolhardy – but that early defeat always left the feeling of a task uncompleted.

A journey around Australia's Highway One would be the answer. The road is known by all Aussies, at least in part, as it runs through every state – even the island of Tasmania – but most people only know their bit and don't take much notice of the rest. Yet it is one of the oldest federal highways in the world, with work having started on it just after the 1901 Act of Federation, long before most people had even heard of cars. At around 17,500 miles, it's also the longest road in a single country in the world.

Australia's founding fathers had wanted this road to tie all the states together, giving the new country and its people a sense of unity and equality, which it did successfully for over one hundred and ten years, but I had heard that in 2010 it was due to be decommissioned as a federal highway. This meant that it would be broken up among the states, with each looking after and developing its own section as it saw fit. The road would largely remain as a physical entity, but would cease to be a single continuous body that united the entire country. No longer would those black and white signs reading simply '1' run like a ribbon around the continent. I knew that I had to travel on it before that happened.

The thought of returning to the land of sharks, snakes and road trains instilled no fear in me; instead my biggest worry was telling my darling wife Catherine of my plans. She was eight months pregnant at the time and I was afraid that this could bring on early labour.

Discretion being the better part of valour, I bravely decided to wait until Geoff and his wife Cate came over for one of our Friday night pizza sessions before breaking the news. I simply announced that I was considering quitting my job, leaving her with an infant and riding off around Australia. Then, as the enormity of what I was saying sunk in, Geoff and I made a bolt for the kitchen.

Once safely out of reach we cracked a couple of tinnies and waited until the screaming stopped,

'I think that went rather well, considering,' said Geoff.

The day after our brilliant brainstorming session – which had involved neither brilliance nor brains – I had phoned Patsy, the head of Blackstaff Press, and suggested the Oz idea to her. She didn't scream and put the phone down like she usually does, which was a good sign, so that evening, I walked up the stairs to the book-lined study at the top of our house, lit the fire, hauled out an atlas and opened it at the map of Australia, with its familiar profile of a schnauzer gazing west. It didn't actually look any bigger than the Isle of Man from my atlas of the British Isles, so it couldn't be that difficult to circumnavigate, I thought.

I got up, poked the fire into life, picked up the phone on my old oak roll-top desk and called Colin to give him a good listening to. Put it this way, Colin is to talking what George Best was to drinking.

'Here, mate, I've been talking to my publishers, and they're on for that idea of a jaunt around Oz on two motorbikes. Do you fancy it?' Then I quietly put the phone down, went downstairs, made a cup of tea, fed the cat, shaved, walked back upstairs and picked up the phone again just in time to hear Colin saying '… so to cut a long story short, I think it's a bloody good idea, mate. I'll just go and break the news to Catherine that we're definitely going to do it. She'll kill me, but it'll be worth it.'

I put down the phone, put the atlas back on the shelf and went downstairs to have a word with Cate, the wife I'd promised never to leave again after being away for three and a half months riding from Chile to Alaska. I found her in the kitchen making fish pie for supper.

'Cate, I was just talking to Colin about another book, and I wanted to see what you thought,' I said.

'Don't tell me: around Australia on two motorbikes,' she said.

I know she's a psychologist, I thought as I went to open a bottle of wine, but it's still spooky how much she knows about what I'm thinking before I've even had a chance to think it.

We filled our glasses and touched them with that old Turkish toast: '*Cam cam'a değil can can'a*' – 'Not glass to glass, but soul to soul'. They met with a bright tinkle, an optimistic sound which drifted out through the French windows and rose into the sky, to join the stars as they looked down on that moment which is one of the rare, perfect moments of life, like the moment when you fall in love, or fling open morning shutters on a new city and go walking into streets fresh with rain, or land an aeroplane so gently that you do not even feel when the wheels touch the ground. The moment when an adventure begins.

Geoff and Colin at the Adelaide Irish Racer Awards before the off, looking presentable for the last time in months.

2

Now all we needed was a sponsor. I hauled out a calculator and a notebook, worked out how much all this was going to cost, then picked up the phone and called Brian Davis, the MD of Nambarrie, who had sponsored the previous expeditions from Delhi to Belfast, and Chile to Alaska.

'Brian, I've got an idea for another adventure, if you fancy sponsoring it,' I said.

'Absolutely.'

'Don't you want to hear where it is, or how much it's going to cost?'

'Not at all. We trust you. Let's have lunch and you can tell me more about it, though.'

'Sure thing. Oh, by the way, because this is going to cost a bit more than previous ones, are you happy enough if I get a secondary sponsor? I was thinking of Adelaide Insurance, since they specialise in motorbikes, and I've met their Nichola Pearce a few times,' I said.

'Not a problem, as long as we get main billing.'

'Absolutely. Can I just say that you're a warm, caring human being, and that tie suits you?'

'Thanks. My wife picked it.'

I put the phone down, and called Nichola, the dynamic, glamorous South African-born head of marketing at Adelaide, and asked to set up a meeting.

Late the next day, I was sitting at a boardroom table with her and the even more dynamic Sam Geddis, who had turned Adelaide from a one-man operation into one of the UK's leading motorbike insurers.

'I have to say to you, Geoff, that I think sponsorship is a complete waste of time,' said Sam, getting things off to a good start. 'TV, radio and newspapers seem to go out of their way to avoid mentioning us, so I've almost given up on the whole idea.'

'Well, here's what Nambarrie got out of the Chile to Alaska adventure,' I said, hauling out of my briefcase a pile of clippings which would have choked a whole family of donkeys and plonking them heavily on the table. A small moth from a species long thought extinct fluttered up from the pile and made its way woozily out of the window into the gathering dusk.

'Well, that is impressive,' said Sam, putting on his glasses and leafing through them. 'OK, now you've got me 40 per cent interested. And when are you thinking of doing this?'

'Spring.'

'Which is our prime time for new business,' said Nichola, endearing me to her for ever.

'True. Now I'm 60 per cent interested. Where are you starting and finishing?'

'Good question.'

He took off his glasses and looked up to where the moth, having decided it was too dark and wet out there, had returned and was headed for the overhead light at a speed that suggested that it was just about to become a myth.

'What about Adelaide to Adelaide with Adelaide?'

'Sam, you're a genius,' I said.

'You're right. And you've got a deal,' he said, reaching across the table and shaking my hand.

Splendid. I had my sponsors. Or so I thought, for like many things that sound too good to be true, it was. Not long after, Nambarrie closed their packing and distribution warehouse in the old Cathedral Quarter of Belfast, leaving only a neatly stacked pyramid of tea chests and the ghostly aroma of first flush Darjeeling in the air to mark a century of history.

Brian lost his job, as did his forty-three staff, and the entire operation disappeared into the bowels of Twinings head-quarters in England. And along with it, it seemed, the plans for Nambarrie Run III: Around Australia on a Triumph.

After several months of trying to find out if Twinings were interested in taking up where Nambarrie left off, I phoned Sam and left a message on his mobile to see if he was interested in being the sole sponsor.

Two minutes later, he texted back with the single word: Yes.

Then, a week later, I was at the opening of IKEA in Belfast when I ran into my old mate Matt Curry, volleyball player turned head of Bluebird, the TV and film production company.

'Oz? Count me in,' he said, when I told him about the plans.

I went back to the office, worked out how much it would cost to bring Matt over as well, and phoned Sam to see if he fancied a TV documentary on the trip as well.

'Absolutely,' he said. I was beginning to like Sam more and more, particularly when Nichola phoned an hour later to say they'd registered a dedicated website, www.adelaideadventures.com, and they'd decided to run a competition that offered anyone who logged on the chance to win a luxury holiday to Australia. Fantastic. Even better, if Colin, Matt and I won the competition, it would save me trying to organise flights. And even if we didn't, I could always fly us out in my microlight one at a time.

That night, I was browsing through assorted Porsche 911s and TVR Chimaeras on the Autotrader website after a couple of glasses of wine, when I came across a lovely Rolls-Royce Silver Shadow for only four and a half grand. Naturally, I mailed Sam immediately to suggest that it would be the perfect support vehicle for the trip, and asked him to come up with an insurance quote for it. Strangely, it was the one time he never replied. It was most unlike him, so I imagine he never got the e-mail.

My job in the meantime, while Geoff was out harassing sponsors, was to try and sort out the actual route we were going to take – a task that was much more difficult than you might think.

There are two things you have to take into consideration when planning to travel anywhere in Australia – the distance and the weather. As Australia has a surface area of almost three million square miles (2,967,909 to be exact), the problem with distance is pretty self-evident, the weather however, is a little harder to predict. It's not just the heat that is the problem – though we do have several kinds, ranging from searing hot and dry, right through to humidity so intense that you need a snorkel just to go for a walk – no, Australians also have to contend with perishing cold; monsoon rains which lead to floods; and winds that will tear your eyeballs out. There are also cyclones, ferocious lightning storms, deadly hailstones the size of cricket balls … and I had to make sure that we avoided the worst of it. Clearly this was going to take some planning. I got out my desk blotter, which is conveniently emblazoned with a large-scale map of Oz, and began to work. Which direction to go was the first big decision that needed to be made.

We needed to make the most of the prevailing winds which cross the continent – in the southern half of the country the winds blow from the south and east making it easier to cross the deserts from east to west – but we also needed to take into consideration the conditions in the tropics up north. We had to try and avoid the intense heat of the southern summer, while also timing it so that we missed the wet season up at the 'top end', as it's known. Just as the enormity of my task threatened to result in me hiding under my desk for the rest of my life, I had a brainwave – I decided to contact the Aussie Bureau of Meteorology and have them tell me what to do.

I got speaking to a really friendly chap there called Wayne who, as well as being an expert on the meshing of the seasons on the continent, also turned out to be an ardent bike lover.

'I love Trumpies,' he said when I told him we were hoping to be able to snag some Triumphs for our trip, 'my old man had a Bonneville when I was a kid. Leaked oil everywhere and was a bastard to start, stop and take around corners, but it was an ace machine. Still love 'em.'

We had a brief but rapturous discussion about motorcycles before I remembered the reason I had called in the first place.

'Wayne, we need to know what time of year and which way to go so that we avoid getting totally fried, boiled, blown away in a cyclone, swept away in a raging torrent, beaten to death by hailstones or trapped for weeks in a flooded desert as crocodiles take us one by one in a bad horror movie pastiche.'

'Starting in Adelaide you reckon? Well then it's gotta be round about February/early March. That way you are coming to the end of the real hot weather down south and then the end of the wet by the time you get up north. The only problem is you might run into the odd cyclone and maybe a flood up there, but you can't have everything.'

'What about direction?' I asked.

'You gotta go west to east. That way you'll get through all the real populated bits on the east coast where the towns and cities will slow you down a bit, and by the time you get up north, the worst of the wet should be over,' he said confirming what I had already thought. 'But there are no guarantees, mate. It's a continent, and you'll get continental weather, the real stuff – not a bit of drizzle and the odd stiff breeze like you blokes over there get all excited about.'

And with that, we had a plan – we would begin the trip the following February.

 Then it was time to sort out a small but significant necessity for riding two motorbikes around Australia; namely, two motorbikes. In other words, it was time to contact the delightful Andrea Friggi at Triumph once more, and hope she'd forgotten that the last time she lent me a bike, I crashed it in Colombia. I wandered upstairs to the study, sat down at the computer and wrote,

> Andrea, stop hiding behind the cupboard: you knew I was going to plague you to help out with another adventure sooner or later.
>
> This one's around Oz next Spring, and the good news is that Adelaide Insurance, the sponsor, have coughed up the extra dosh for Matt Curry, head of Bluebird TV and film production company, to come out and make a documentary. Matt's applying for an Innovations Grant which he's pretty confident of getting, which will mean a full production crew and possibly a series with celebrity presenter.
>
> It'll be like Ewan and Charley, only with more talent and less money.
>
> The other main difference is that I'm doing it with fellow author and biker Colin O'Carroll, who was born here but grew up there, so the plan is for us to both to write the series and book, me from the point of view of an Oz novice and him from the point of view of returning to the land of his lost youth.
>
> In practical terms, that means two bikes, which can be demo, second-hand, or ones lying down the back of a dealership in Oz. Sam Geddis, the MD of Adelaide, is planning to join us for the first two weeks, so if he could beg, steal or borrow a bike, even better.

She replied before the end of the day.

> Hi Geoff,
>
> They took all our cupboards away so there's nowhere left to hide.
>
> My Oz colleagues have confirmed that in principle they can loan you two Tigers for your trip. However they have asked if you will have insurance in place to cover the bikes in the unlikely (we hope!) event they are written off.
>
> We can also provide gear for the trip – could you let me

know what you think you'll need – both for the bikes, such as panniers and top boxes, and for the riders – and I'll arrange.

We'll provide a bike for Sam, and gear with at least 50 per cent discount.

Splendid. Mind you, I should have asked her if she could make sure the bikes were fitted with wombat scoops, like old American locomotives, because the morning after, I came across a piece in *The Times* about James Bowthorpe, who'd just become the fastest man to cycle around the world in spite of an ambush in Iran, food poisoning in India and, most disturbing of all, a collision with a wombat in Oz.

'Everyone thinks ooh, wombats, they sound cute, and when the Australians warned me to look out for them at night, I laughed them off,' he told *The Times*. 'Sure enough, I hit one going downhill at speed into a town called Eden. They're massive, it was like hitting a brick wall. My bike folded up and I went flying over the handlebars. The wombat ran off and I limped into town, luckily with only scratches and bruises.'

Thankfully, the next day, Henry Rivers Fletcher, the PR for Schuberth, said he'd provide us with free helmets, which were presumably wombat-resistant, and the day after that, Colin, Matt and I met Sam and Nichola at Adelaide, along with Gavin Livingston, the artist who'd done the covers of my books and who was going to produce all the artwork for the trip. It was like *The Magnificent Seven*, except without all the dead Mexicans.

By the end of the meeting, I had told them about the clothing and helmets, and we'd decided on the design of the stickers to go on the bikes. Free gear and stickers. For a bloke, it didn't get much better.

Even better, Etihad Airways said they'd fly the team out to Oz; Duke Video said they were keen on world distribution and marketing rights for Matt's DVD; and both the BBC and Channel 4 said they'd be interested in broadcasting it, followed a day later by Setanta – presumably because since losing Premiership football they now had several hundred hours to fill.

Except that now we had koalas to worry about as well as wombats, if an e-mail I got from fellow journalist Joanne Savage was anything to go by.

Good luck on the biking round Australia with Colin. I will certainly tune in to watch the recorded results; the pair of you are wild, iconoclastic men of speed!

I've never been Down Under but it is bound to be unmercifully hot and koala bears are apparently much more vicious than they seem - or perhaps I am confusing them with pandas? Anyway, it all sounds fearfully exciting to me and you are bound to have an exquisitely unpredictable adventure.

Seize the fish!

Making a note to ask Triumph if we could get leather jackets with 'Wild, Iconoclastic Men of Speed' on the back, I wrote back to Joanne telling her about how, according to Colin, wombats slept in the middle of the road because it was warm, and if their alarm didn't go off, they were still there when an unsuspecting chap came motorcycling along to find a furry, horny speed bump in the middle of the road. Result: bits of man and motorcycle scattered across the road, while the wombat scratches itself and mutters, 'Good heavens, what was that? I say, look at the time. I'd better be getting on with wombat things, whatever they are.'

'The thing is,' said Colin a few days later, 'wombats aside, it doesn't matter how good a biker you are, it's all the other prats on the road who might kill you.'

'Not if we see them first,' I said, 'which funny enough is one of the main things I was taught when I did my Institute of Advanced Motorists car test a few years ago – to always create the biggest possible safe zone around and in front of you.'

'Which is what?'

'The distance you can see, basically. If you increase this area it means you can actually drive faster when it's safe to do so, since you should always drive so you can stop in the distance you can see. I found it really useful.'

'There's only one thing for it, then. We should do our IAM advanced bike test before we go,' said Colin.

'Aye, I was thinking you'd say that,' I said, helping myself to another beer, mine having mysteriously evaporated.

The next day, I got on the phone to the local branch of the IAM, and a fortnight later Colin and I found ourselves standing with Paul Sheldon, police motorcyclist turned advanced instructor.

'Geoff, do you remember the system of control from your car test?' he said.

'Sure do. It's engraved on my mind like acid on steel: mirror, course, signal, speed, gear, horn if necessary and manoeuvre. And I guess on a bike you'd stick lifesaver, the look over your shoulder, just before manoeuvre.'

'Very impressive. Shame they've changed it all to Information, Position, Speed, Gear, Acceleration.'

'Listen, I'll never learn all that. Can I just stick to the old system?'

'Aye, same difference. And it's not called a lifesaver any more. It's a blind-spot check. Right, let's go riding. Stick these earphones in your helmets so I can talk to you.'

We set off, with first Colin, then me, taking the lead and Paul behind. I don't know about Colin, but with an ex-police biker watching my every move, I was riding like a granny on Valium. After half an hour, Paul pulled us in for a natter.

'Right, you both need to ride faster. There's no point being on a bike if you don't make progress by overtaking and filtering past slow-moving traffic. Colin, you could be faster through corners as well, and Geoff, you seem obsessed with riding down the middle of the road,' he said.

'Listen, the first LP I bought was Neil Diamond's *Twelve Greatest Hits*, and I've been middle of the road ever since,' I said lamely, and we set off again, making progress, filtering furiously, making our way to the front of the queue at traffic lights, and generally behaving like well-mannered kings of the road. Especially since we'd just been told by an ex-cop to ride faster.

Over the next few weeks, Paul tweaked and corrected, admonished and praised. We knew we were finally getting it right when long periods went by without a word in our earphones. And when he told us we were ready for our test.

The following Saturday morning, after a sleep disturbed by nightmares that I had forgotten not only the advanced stuff, but how to ride a bike at all, I turned up, yawning mightily, to find Charlie Stewart, the examiner, in disturbingly bright and breezy form.

'Right, let's go. You and Colin are the third and fourth I've done this week, and I usually fail one in four,' he grinned.

'Thanks for that, Charlie,' I grinned back, and we set off for an hour and a half of intense riding under the equally intense gaze of Charlie.

'Yes, nice safe, systematic ride. I'll tell you if you've passed once I get back,' he said when we arrived back at the start point to find Colin anxiously awaiting his turn.

'I may as well follow you around then, since I'm doing nothing else,' I said.

Ninety minutes later, we were back and identifying road signs from Charlie's flip chart as a final theory test.

'Well, I'm pleased to tell you that you've both passed. Your certificates will be in the post,' he said at last, and we shook his hand and rode home, smug in the knowledge that not only had we reduced our chances of having an accident by 85 per cent, but earned a nice little discount on our insurance.

 In the meantime, we had started to put together an itinerary of things we wanted to see and do, people we wanted to meet and film in Australia, and estimated what our average travelling distance would be each day. In the end we were able to work out that it was going to take us between ten and twelve weeks to get all the way around.

Realising that this would be a costly business, I decided to take a chance and call the Australian Tourist Board to see if they could help us out. I excitedly explained our plans to a charming woman based in London who agreed that it was an adventure and a half, but told me that they had already spent their budget.

'I tell you what,' she said, upon hearing my disappointed protests, 'we're the federal tourism board but you could try approaching the individual states you're travelling through – they might be able to do something for you.'

'Brilliant!' I cried, already reaching for my keyboard to start bombarding the states with electronic begging letters. In the end only Western Australia, South Australia and Victoria were able to help us, but boy did they – offering us accommodation, tours, wildlife safaris and visits to aboriginal lands. It was all done with a minimum of fuss or demands and with a superabundance of efficiency and good humour. All they asked was that we write fairly honestly about the attractions of visiting – hardly an ethical dilemma, I thought, as I had a fair idea about some of the wonderful things we would see and do.

In the end it was arranged that we would take in all the usual big capital cities, but would also visit various music and art festivals, motorcycle events and museums, coral reefs, wildlife sanctuaries, rainforests and of course beaches – lots and lots of beaches. I couldn't wait to show off the country of my youth to my companions.

By now other ideas were coming thick and fast. Most of the thick ones came from me, and the fast ones came from people like Colin Paterson of IAM, who had been designated as the official charity for the trip, who suggested not only a tracking device for the bikes so that anyone clicking onto the website could see where we were, but a web cam for a live feed. Then we realised that the only audience would be insomniacs, since we'd be riding during the day in Oz, which was night time in the UK.

Also shot down, sadly, was the idea of Matt's seven-year-old daughter Rose that we bolt a sidecar to one of the bikes so that her dad could film from it.

'Wonderfully mad idea, but we don't do sidecars,' was the understandable response of Triumph's endlessly patient Andrea. Naturally, Matt was devastated, not to mention Rose, but I comforted them with the thought that we could always make one out of used Foster's tins once we got there and gaffer tape it on.

In any case, Matt and I soon forgot about sidecars and web cams, since the next day we were down at Phillip McCallan's, the Triumph dealer and former race ace, with Sam and the perpetually glamorous Nichola from Adelaide Insurance, sorting out important stuff like where all the stickers and cameras would go on the bikes and helmets, when Daniel Day-Lewis walked through the door.

He'd driven up from his home in Wicklow with his mate John McHugo to road-test the new KTM RC8R, and he turned out to be the most charming and decent chap imaginable, as we stood for the next hour drinking coffee and chatting about bikes. Even better, he happily agreed to wish me all the best for the trip on camera, for which I was so grateful I told him that if Danny De Vito didn't take up the offer to play me in the movie about the trip, he was next in line.

'You're a bit late,' said Cate when I walked into the house later that afternoon. 'Everything OK?'

'Yes, just been swanning about with my new special best friend Daniel Day-Lewis,' I said, telling her what had happened.

'Honestly, you're turning into more of a luvvie every day. Maybe you could feed the cats when you return to earth,' she said.

Still, at least she didn't bring me back to reality as much as Sam Geddis did when I phoned to tell him about meeting the star.

'Didn't he do that film *My Big Foot*?' said Sam.

 It was round about this time that I considered the possibility of getting a fuel sponsor and decided to contact oil company Ampol, a peculiarly Aussie outfit that was actually owned by the motoring public and which aimed simply to provide affordable and reliable fuel everywhere in the country. I had worked at an Ampol garage all through high school, and it was there that I gained most of my mechanical knowledge. I could be found there most weekends, stripping down one of my motorcycles in an attempt to get it to go even faster.

I contacted Ampol HQ to ask them if they would be willing to provide us with the fuel we needed on our journey.

'Sorry mate,' I was told, 'we're owned by a Yank oil company now. Ampol's just a sign on the forecourt.'

Undeterred, I gave the parent company a bell, but was disappointed once again when they too turned down my request.

'No worries chum,' said Geoff when I broke the bad news. 'I've budgeted for fuel and then some, so we'll get around no bother.'

With my first-hand knowledge of the vast distances we would be traversing, I was still a little uneasy, but I was mollified by Geoff's breezy confidence and bewildering display of budget figures – we would be fine.

 About a week later, Matt, Colin and I got together over a few pre-Christmas beers to have a natter about story ideas, finance and the like.

'You know,' said Matt, 'the one big expense we haven't taken care of is the back-up vehicle for the film crew, which is going to be about four grand out of the budget.'

'Get Baron Blag on the case,' said Colin, draining his third beer and looking pointedly in my direction. 'So far he's managed to blag sponsorship, bikes, flights and kit, so a car shouldn't be a problem.'

'Easy peasy. Any suggestions, apart from the usual ones like Hertz and Avis?'

'There are a couple in Oz who do slightly older cars, like Rent-A-Wreck and Rent-A-Bomb,' said Colin.

'Rent-A-Bomb. I love it. Leave it to me.'

The next morning, I wrote to Rent-A-Bomb asking if they fancied lending us a vehicle, but just as I sent the e-mail, Matt phoned.

'Here, I've found a company called Wicked Campers, who do these mad hippy camper vans. They're four-wheel drive, and they come with a kitchen and beds, if you want to be boringly practical about it,' he said. 'More importantly, each van is painted a different colour, their website has a van being driven by a koala with a kangaroo leaning out of the window smoking a spliff, and if you turn up naked, you get your first day free. Unless you're over sixty, in which you get the first day free for keeping your clothes on.'

'I love it. Especially the naked bit. Do you think they'd be interested?'

'I'll tell you how interested they are. I've just e-mailed them, and the boss John Webb phoned back to say he's a biker himself and he'd love to.'

I logged onto the Wicked website to check out the naked customers, and found the company philosophy: 'We believe in the experience of the road trip. It can change the way you see yourself, the world, and the world around you. It's about getting something out of the journey itself, rather than worrying about how fast you can get to your destination; what's the hurry? A road trip is a philosophy of life, a way of learning about yourself, an experience, a way to test yourself, a way to grow up ... the possibilities are endless.'

I liked the sound of that as well. Except maybe for the bit about growing up.

Two days later, however, I got an e-mail from Colin, who'd found this on an Australian news website:

All but four of a fleet of 86 popular backpacker hire camper vans have been pulled off Queensland's roads because they are not roadworthy. Wicked Campers voluntarily withdrew seventy-seven of their fleet and submitted the remaining nine for roadworthy tests, but only four passed … the December investigation took place after random compliance checks at Wicked Campers' outlets in August and October in Cairns. The results in Cairns prompted inspectors to investigate the company on a state-wide basis. Mechanical faults included structural rust, defective seating, oil leaks and severe accident damage.

Still, as a man who had once ridden a Royal Enfield back from Delhi, structural rust, defective seating, oil leaks and severe accident damage were par for the course.

In any case, I had a spare pair of dongles with me this time courtesy of Wicklow woman Josephine Dinan, who I'd met when her daughter Mary came to Belfast to interview me for a book on travel writers. I found her to be completely bonkers, even at first sight, but in the best possible way. And my assessment was confirmed when one morning two weeks before departure, I got a package from her with a card saying: 'Dear Geoff, I have read *The Road to Gobblers Knob* and it's brilliant, but as you seem to be at risk of losing your dongles, I am enclosing a spare pair.'

And she did: a pair of hand-knitted ones that looked disturbingly realistic, accompanied by a footnote from Mary saying, 'Mum says you can hang the dongles on the handlebars of your bike. They are designer dongles, so they are unique. Two of a kind. And here's a little limerick for you.

> A biker called Geoff down in Oz,
> had a limp down under because,
> his dongles had been knitted,
> and were badly fitted,
> and his dongles got covered in moss.'

Splendid. I could use them in case I lost mine, along with my marbles, and as a weapon to fend off rabid wombats.

In the meantime, people kept asking me if I was looking forward to the trip, and I kept telling them the same thing: that my adventures always seemed like an exercise in theoretical logistics until the moment I was sitting on the bike thinking, 'Oh my God, it's happened again. What am I doing here?'

And adventures are like Christmas, in that it seems ages away and then suddenly it's Christmas Eve with not a turkey wrapped or a present stuffed. As a result, everything suddenly started to happen in fast forward.

The www.adelaideadventures.com website went live, and I immediately got slagged senseless by everyone who visited the site and saw the video clip in which I rode off on a Tiger with the side stand down.

I can't quite understand how I did it, since I thought Triumph had idiot-proof technology in place which would cut out the engine if you put it into gear with the stand down. Obviously a big enough idiot can beat any system. I did try to pretend that I left the stand down deliberately so that if I got tired while going around a left-hand bend, I could stop, prop the bike up while I had a brief snooze, and then proceed, but in spite of the fact that I had been a journalist for years, and therefore dedicated to telling the truth at all costs, no one believed me.

Thankfully, Colin diverted all the attention to himself a few days later when he took his new Schuberth helmet out for a test ride, called around after a couple of hours, and said, 'This visor's crap, mate. I can't see a bloody thing out of it.'

'That's because you've left the protective plastic film on, you pillock,' I said sympathetically.

He removed it just in time, since the next day we had to ride two Tigers up a steep ramp onto a stage at the Adelaide Motorcycle Festival press conference to launch the trip. I led the way, then flinched as there was a loud bang. 'Bloody hell,' I thought, 'I've hit something,' only for the air to be filled with silver ticker-tape.

Naturally, I then parked the bike so close to the podium that I couldn't get off. And left the lights on.

'Why are you going anti-clockwise?' said one journalist once the conference was well under way. 'Is it because of the prevailing winds, or because it means you go through the civilised bits first rather than heading straight into the Nullarbor Desert?'

'No, it's because we're riding on the left, so it'll be shorter. All we have to do is keep the sharks on the right, and the kangaroos on the left, and we won't get lost,' I said.

Still, it all went well, and afterwards we were even mobbed by groupies. Well, one groupie. And she was a pensioner. 'Never mind, you have to start somewhere,' I thought as I rode off the stage and nearly ran into the stand run by Nick Sanders, the legendary biker who'd set several records for the fastest time around the world by riding his Yamaha R1 one thousand miles a day and only stopping for occasional catnaps on the bike, sometimes even when it was stationary. Not surprisingly, his hair always looks like he's just taken his helmet off after wearing it all day.

'Sorry about that, Nick,' I said, going over to him after I got off the bike.

'No worries, mate,' he said, shaking my hand.

'Listen, anything we should look out for in Oz?'

'Wombats. Like hitting a brick wall,' he said.

See? I told you I wasn't being paranoid.

Naturally, I e-mailed Triumph immediately to say that having those wombat scoops fitted to the bikes was now looking more crucial than ever. Only to be told by Colin, 'A cowcatcher won't work – it tends to lift them up by the pouch so you have an extremely irate marsupial with very sharp claws hanging off the front of your bike.'

Ho hum. In the meantime, there was even worse news from Mal Jarrett of Triumph's Australian importers.

It's not the wombats that you have to worry about, it's the emus! Next to sheep, they're known to be the dumbest animals that God ever put life into. They run at 60–80kph beside you before suddenly changing direction … straight in front of you!

The good news is that if you hit them at just the right speed they'll deflect off your fairing and spin down the side of your bike, giving it a nice clean as they do so, sort of like going through an automated car wash. Then there are the snakes which like to sunbathe on the roads, and don't get me started on the kangaroos ... happy travels.

I decided to stop reading my e-mails after that, and went upstairs to pack my kit, thinking as I did that the only object that had survived all the adventures of Delhi to Belfast, Chicago to LA and Chile to Alaska was my watch, a Casio I'd bought for a tenner because I didn't want to risk losing my good one.

I hauled it out of the drawer of my desk, and it was still ticking away, after twelve years on the original battery.

Gloria, Colin, Geoff and Sam on the South Australian Coast

3

Adventures always begin at dawn.

Or, to be more precise, standing in the Belfast rain at four in the morning waiting for the bus to Dublin Airport with Colin and our enormous film crew of Matt and his cousin Gareth McGrillan.

'Everybody got everything?' asked Matt. 'Passport, ticket, money, driving licence?'

'Driving licence?' I said, realising two things simultaneously: that I had left it on the hall table, and that I was just about to ride fifteen thousand miles around a country with no proof that I was capable of doing so. Still, at least for the first time ever I had insurance, courtesy of Adelaide's Sam Geddis, who met us at the airport. With him was his wife Gloria who, in a dazzling triumph of style over grim reality, and despite the fact that it was six in the morning, was wearing an outfit which wouldn't have looked out of place at Henley Regatta.

I found it easy to leave freezing cold, wet Belfast. Even getting up at 3 a.m. was a doddle, but it was much harder to leave my darling little family. Neither Cathy nor I slept well on the last night before the 'off', so after a final cuddle and some last tender words like 'If you get killed, I'll bloody murder you,' I slipped out of my nice warm bed and quietly got dressed.

I couldn't resist having a look in on my two-year-old daughter Ella Rose. Born in September 2007 – which goes to show you the time it took for me and Geoff to go from adventure-planning stage to actual execution! – she has the most loving nature of any child her age, paradoxically coupled with rapidly developing meglomania.

Unusually, she was awake, and she just looked up at me with her big blue eyes, a quizzical expression on her face and whispered, 'Daddy'. Holding back the tears, and trying to disguise the tremor in my voice, I tucked her in and shushed her back to sleep, before tiptoeing out of her bedroom for the last time for three months.

As I grabbed my gear and headed out, closing the front door behind me, it really hit home – the time had finally arrived … the pipe dream was no more … this was for real. I'd left my job and was now leaving my family to undertake this journey.

'Whose big idea was this?' I thought to myself as I lugged my bags to the taxi. 'That's right – mine,' I remembered.

On the bus down to Dublin, after some compulsory manly banter with Geoff, Matt and Gareth we all retreated into our own little worlds.

Exhausted, yet too wired to sleep, I could only really think about my loved ones, but as the sky lightened and the city came into view, my thoughts slowly turned to the adventure ahead.

We took off, and for the first half hour I pressed every button on the entertainment system and kept coming back to a tone-deaf mullah chanting the Koran. Just as I was about to become the world's first Church of Ireland fundamentalist terrorist and attack the stewardess with the remote control, I gave up, read the instructions and found the Western classical channel. I mean, no harm to Mohammed and all that, but Bach does far better tunes.

I watched *Memoirs of a Geisha* then listened to Eurythmics' *Greatest Hits*, which made me feel a strange combination of Japanese and young again, then curled up as best I could and tried to get some sleep. It seemed like I had hardly nodded off before we were landing.

Our first and only stop was Abu Dhabi, a place I had been several times before but not in almost thirty years. In the 1970s it had been a relatively poor place, and the vista flying in was sand in every direction, with the tracks of Bedouin and their camel caravans clearly visible from the air.

I recall getting off the plane with a couple of other hardy souls, just to stretch our legs and look around. There wasn't much to see back then, as the terminal was nothing more than a glorified converted hangar surrounded by sand dunes, and I remember having a brief moment of panic when I noticed that on every bench were bodies wrapped head to toe in sheets. I'd had a sudden, horrific thought that there must have been a major crash and that the terminal was being used a a temporary morgue. But then one of the 'bodies' sat up, scratched, grunted and lay back down again and I quickly realised that they were just the local transit passengers waiting for the next flight.

I remember making my way over to the hospitality area, which in the seventies was located in a roped-off corner of the terminal, where I ordered one of their criminally expensive beers, and was served by a very dishevelled waiter who would have fitted in perfectly in a Sergio Leone spaghetti western. Thirst quenched, I waved goodbye to the corpses and returned to the aircaft for the next long leg of my flight.

How times have changed. Abu Dhabi now rivals its near-neighbour Dubai for glitz and glamour, with the new airport being both visually stunning and incredibly efficient. The skyline is filled with architecturally groundbreaking buildings and the island blazes with light. Our airline Etihad has even based its world hub there and as one wag put it, they've gone 'from camels to Cadillacs in one generation'.

Now it was only a short hop before we would be landing in Australia.

'Good day, sir. What's the purpose of your visit to Australia?' said the red-headed immigration official at the Melbourne airport. I knew he was bluffing, because I'd read enough Oz travel guides, including *Twisting Throttle*, Mike Hyde's hilarious book about riding around the country, to know that Aussies didn't talk like that. As Hyde had helpfully pointed out, Aussies greet each other with 'Hair gamay?' as shorthand for 'How you going, mate?' and bid farewell with 'Sluddermay' for 'See you later, mate'. It was a test, like when the German officer said 'Good luck' to Gordon Jackson just as he was getting on the bus in *The Great Escape*. And I was up to the occasion.

'G'Day, Blue. Hair gamay. Well, me and me mates here, we're going to ride a couple of Triumphs from Adelaide through Crow Eater and Mexican country then up through Banana Bender land and beyond the black stump to the Never Never, then down through Sandgroper territory and home.'

'And where are you planning to stay, sir?'

'We're going to ride to the end of the arvo, mate, maybe having a few Vegemite snackies on the road, then stop by a billabong, roll out our swags, whip on the Speedos, go for a dip, keeping a good dekko for salties, shout each other a few stubbies of XXXX grog from the Esky in the back of the ute, get a few snags and yabbies on the barbie, have a yabber and a last slash down the dunny, then get our heads down on the nearest gibber and nod off under the stars rapt with the warm fuzzies.'

'You coming the raw prawn with me, mate?' he said.

'Nah, it's fair dinkum, mate. Ridgi-didge, straight up, cross me heart and hope to die.'

'Good on ya, mate,' he said, reaching across and shaking my hand, 'Sludder.'

'Sluddermay,' I said, picking up my bag and preparing to walk away.

'Oh, just one final thing ...'

My heart froze. Was everything to fail, at this final hour? 'Yes, mate?' I asked.

'Do you have a criminal record?'

I sighed with relief, and reached into my bag, 'I didn't think it was necessary any longer, mate, but I brought this just in case,' I said, handing him a CD of Daniel O'Donnell's *The Christmas Album*. He took it gingerly from me, then tossed it into the bin.

'That's crim enough for me, mate. Hope she'll be apples for ya.'

I shook his hand again for good measure, and was just walking towards the exit when I felt a hand on my shoulder. I froze, fearing I had been caught at the last minute for only pretending I liked Vegemite, only to hear the familiar voice of Colin, as if from a distance.

'Wake up mate, we're landing in Melbourne in ten minutes. Are you all right?'

I looked groggily around, and realised we were still on the plane. 'Aye. I just had this mad dream that we'd already landed,' I said, rubbing the sleep from my eyes.

We made our way off the plane and into the airport, where the officials took only a cursory glance at our passports, wished us a good stay in Oz, and sent us on our way. Switching our water-down-the-plughole setting to clockwise and the intonation at the end of our sentences to Up rather than Down, we stepped out of the terminal into the balmy heat of a Melbourne evening.

We found a hotel, checked in, and three things happened in quick succession. First of all we looked at a map and discovered that Australia was very big. Then we realised that the events we'd planned for the first few days – namely lawnmower racing and a big salt-lake drag racing event – were in places so far away that it would take us most of the three months planned for the trip to get there. Finally, one of Matt's brand-new high-resolution cameras chose that moment to refuse to work.

So with nothing to do and no way to film it, we did the only thing possible: cracked open the bottle of Bundaberg rum Colin had bought at the airport, had a mug, and went to bed.

By the time we got onto the plane for the short hop to Adelaide the next morning, I had become convinced that the Australian Government was putting Prozac in the water, since every single person we had met since we arrived had been unfailingly cheery, optimistic and helpful. Including the drug-sniffer dog at the airport. It was an impression confirmed by the fact that among the duty-free items for sale in the Qantas in-flight magazine was a guitar, presumably in case everyone on board fancied a good old sing-song.

However, that discovery was not the highlight of the day. It was not even picking up the back-up vehicle, a Toyota Hiace High Top with 652,425km on the clock which the chaps at Wicked Campers had painted up for us with an inspired combination of bike adventure graphics and rude quotations.

No, it was the moment when we collected the keys of two Tigers from the Triumph dealer in Adelaide, started up the engine and I heard that sweet hum which had accompanied me all the way from Chile to Alaska on my previous adventure, and was again in this moment the sound of freedom and the open road.

Once we got ourselves organised, we decided to visit the state migration museum to look into the experiences of the people who built this modern, vibrant, yet traditional society.

Southern Australia holds a unique position in the country's history, being the only colony never to accept convicts and having been set up as a new-world utopia in 1836. The glaring stain on that great ideal being that only white British people were allowed in. That exclusivity didn't last too long though as the new settlers soon found that it was hard to lie around all day thinking idealistic utopian thoughts and creating new philosophies if there was no one around to make the cucumber sandwiches and iron the sheets, so other 'less pure' races were eventually allowed in to do the real work.

That being said, the state has, in its past, made many significant social and political leaps, putting it ahead of its fellow states and indeed the world. It was the first place in the world to give women full voting rights; it has a tradition of encouraging the arts and artists; and back in the 1970s, under charismatic and urbane premier Don Dunstan, it took radical steps to de-criminalise the use of drugs. Homosexuality was also de-criminalised and a more liberal attitude to sexual preferences in general engendered an attitude which gradually spread over the state's borders resulting in the mostly tolerant, and certainly legally equal, situation that prevails today.

It was a welcome respite to get out of the blazing sun and into the museum which is located in Adelaide's university quarter. Curator Deirdre Robb welcomed us with, what we were now getting used to as, the familiar warm SA greeting, and gave us a potted history of the state and of the museum itself. The building was at one time a 'school' for aboriginal children who had been forcibly removed from their families to be Christianised and trained to act as servants and workers for the settlers. That scheme didn't last too long though as the aboriginal parents soon realised that they were losing their families as well as their land. So many took their children back, and fled.

The building then became a home for the destitute – a term which included not only the mad and the bad but also poor, unmarried women who'd fallen pregnant, many of them through being abused by their masters. Deirdre informed us that these women were treated tolerably well for the times and that many went on to lead very successful lives.

However, it was a recently opened special exhibit which struck a particular chord with me. It was all about the 'Ten Pound Tourists' and, for me, it indicated that there is now some recognition of the harm this scheme caused in the past. The Australian and British governments now admit their roles in what can now be seen at best as an ill-conceived strategy and at worst, modern slavery.

Thousands of children had been shipped out to work as part of this colonisation scheme, and some became little more than indentured servants for sometimes sadistic and perverted employers. They were robbed of their childhood, their families, their culture and any sense of themselves as persons of worth.

People had been sold the dream of a new life – a life in which they would own their own home and car, spend their days at the beach, and generally live the life of a beach-bum millionaire. But, for many the reality was totally different and they arrived, full of hope, only to be taken to live in crudely constructed migrant camps – many of them located in dry, barren areas – facing hardships of heat, dust, flies and all the other hazards this strange land brought with it.

Many of the exhibits in the museum, which included images of people struggling to come to terms with their new home, were achingly familiar to me, as I recalled my family's own struggles, both physical and emotional, as we first began to settle in our new home. There were many fond memories too though. In many ways I'd had an idyllic childhood and adolescence, and I was proud that I had a connection to this great country.

But as I stepped out of the museum and into the sunshine, I pulled myself back to the present. Tonight we were heading to the city centre park where Groupe F, the same company that put on the globe-stopper at the Sydney Olympics, were putting on a spectacular fireworks display to mark the start of the fiftieth Adelaide Arts festival – one of the biggest festivals in the world and one which has given South Australia a reputation as 'the Festival State'.

Having successfully lost Geoff on the way, after he chickened out at an amber light, we did a circuit of the former Grand Prix track before finding the huge park set for the big launch. As the lights dimmed, the disembodied voice of an elder of the aboriginal Gharna tribe welcomed us on to what is their traditional land. In a speech made all the more meaningful after the very belated apology from the white settler population of Australia for the things their forebears had done, she said, 'Let us not dwell on the bad things of the past, but let us not forget the past, and now, let us walk on together in harmony.' The words were met with sustained and respectful applause.

My faith in the natural Australian disrespect for authority was restored though when the South Australian Minister for the Arts then appeared to formally open the festival and was greeted with a chorus of sighs, groans and occasional catcalls.

At one stage in the glare of a starburst of rockets, I thought I saw Geoff lit up like the white bark of a snowgum lurking behind a tree, but dismissed the notion as a trick of the bush and, as the 45-minute spectacular drew to a close, Matt and I – along with several million others – decided to steal a march and get away.

I was reminded again of the sheer size of this country and the space available to all as the crowds melted away into the night, the giant park allowing everyone to make their way out with no pushing, shoving, or even the slightest hint of a rush.

After Colin had hurtled through the first amber light, leaving me stranded at the red, I had found the city centre, the park and the thousands of people waiting for the fireworks display, but of Colin there was no sign. Still, never mind. I found a space all to myself in the throng and settled down to watch the show, only to find that the reason I had the space all to myself was because the largest tree in Adelaide, and possibly all of Australia, was directly between me and the display.

As a result, half an hour of inspired pyrotechnics was reduced to a dim cacophony of bangs and flickerings, in much the same way as I imagine someone in, say, Marseille, might have experienced a bombardment on the Western Front. Sighing deeply, I rode back to where we were staying, only to realise that Colin had the key and I couldn't even let myself in. Still, nothing like sitting on the pavement looking at the moon to bring out the Zen Buddhist in you, and I was in a state of complete inner calm when Colin finally appeared with a cheery grin an hour later.

'I don't know, bloody first rule of biking in pairs, if you go through a bloody amber light, check in the bloody mirror to see if your mate's stuck at the bloody red light, then bloody well stop and wait for him,' I said, strangling him just as cheerily.

'Sorry about that, mate. Do try and keep up next time. Fancy a beer?'

'Right first time. Lead the way,' I said, safe in the knowledge that the pub was only 100 yards away, and there were no traffic lights on the way.

In the middle of the night, I was woken by Colin rummaging around in the bottom of his bag, 'Starving, mate. Can't find the sausage sarnie I made before I left Belfast. I usually keep one under the bed at home for emergencies like this,' he muttered. 'Ah, here it is. In the last place you look, as usual.'

'Has to be by definition, chum, since after you find something, you stop looking.'

'Good point, Bruce,' he said, tucking into his sausage buttie with some fervour.

Early the next morning, a Sunday, we rang the director of the national motor museum in nearby Birdwood to see if we could swing by in the afternoon and do some filming. The answer, as with everywhere in Australia, was an instant yes. You got the feeling that if you phoned up the Prime Minister at six on Christmas morning and asked if you could pop over to interview him naked in the swimming pool, he'd say, 'No worries, mate. I'll get the wife to stick an extra few prawns on the barbie.'

Having sorted that out, we turned to the most important part of the whole expedition: what to call our vehicles.

'What about Wicked Willie for the van?' I said.

'Actually, I'd like to call her Matilda, because that was the name of the van my wife went around Oz in with her mates before we met, and the name we gave to our daughter because of that,' said Matt, the old softie.

'Matilda it is. Now we need a name for the woman on the sat nav who tells us where to go,' said Gareth.

'What about Nichola, Sam's trusty head of marketing, since she's always telling us where to go back home?' said Colin.

Perfect. I decided to call my Triumph Jim after the imaginary rabbit in *Way To Go*, and Colin decided on Rosie, so that the pair were Rosie and Jim after the children's TV series, which seemed appropriate.

Well, it wasn't just the kids TV show that inspired the name, though as the bikes were a pair and we were like two big kids let loose in a sweetie shop, it was apt. She was also to be called Rosie after the legendary AC/DC song, 'Whole Lotta Rosie' as she was a big powerful girl, and lastly, but most importantly, after my little girl Ella Rose. When I announced the news that my Tiger was nameless no more, the choice was widely applauded, especially by Matt, whose little girl is also Rosie, and who in common with me, he was missing very much.

So with our bikes stickered up and my spare dongles dangling from Matilda's rear-view mirror, we were ready to go. Ahead of us lay fifteen thousand miles of road, which was a long way to go to end up back where we started.

But it is the journey, not the destination, which counts, and anyway, as any Irishman knows, the longest distance between two points is a straight line, as proved by one of the most famous Irishmen of all, Albert Einstein, when he showed that space was curved. This is a phenomenon familiar to anyone trying to find the way back to their seat in the pub after going to the toilet. Theoretically, according to Einstein's hypothesis at least, if you look out into space and your eyesight is good enough, you should be able see the back of your head, although since the light will take a bit of time making the journey, you may have lost a bit of hair in the meantime.

And so, the back of our heads firmly in our sights, we started our engines and rode off in the sure and certain knowledge that we would eventually meet ourselves coming back, and be able to find out what a good time we'd had.

By lunchtime, after winding our way into the hills surrounding the city, we were wandering around the myriad joys of the motor museum with a chap called Steve Farrer. Look, there was a Rover P6 3500 exactly like the one I bought once for £130 in pouring rain at midnight in a loyalist estate in Belfast, for no other reason than that I'd fallen in love with the walnut dashboard with its row of dials with flickering needles, and the gloriously visceral burble of the V8 engine. And the fact that I'd had a few. I'd installed a hi-fi in it, which cost twice as much as the car, and cruised around in it all summer until the fuel bills finally bankrupted me, since it did fourteen miles to the gallon on a good day.

And look, there were the Nortons and Rudges that my dear old dad and his brother Fred had raced in the fifties, before Dad married Mum, and Fred met Ina working in a haberdashery.

He'd called in every day to see her on the pretext of buying thread, and by the time he plucked up the courage to ask her out, he'd amassed 180 spools. Heavens, the museum even had the same model of Velocette that they'd taken on their honeymoon, and which was so underpowered that when they came to any hills Ina had to get off and walk up. It was beginning to feel as if this wasn't a motor museum, more a museum of not only my own life, but that of my forebears.

On the way out, I bought a Triumph badge, pinned it to my

lapel and stepped out into the late-afternoon heat, overcome by emotions so poignant and complex that I could hardly begin to express them.

I too found the day to be more overwhelming than anticipated. The museum was as much of a revelation for me as it had been for Geoff, mostly because of the collection of old cars from the sixties and seventies. There were models of Holdens, Fords, Valiants and countless others which took me back to my teenage years, and reminded me of people that have long since gone either out of my life or out of this world.

I thought of drive-in movies spent in the back of a panel van, of 'hotted-up' muscle cars driven by some of my more macho mates, and of surfing safaris down the coast, sleeping in a station wagon and trying a new beach every day. It was hard to believe that I was once that skinny kid of my memory, in love with the outdoor life when every weekend was an adventure, but then I reflected that there must be some of him still left in me, as here I was, back again, about to ride around the rim of this vast country.

By early evening, we were riding through rolling downs punctuated by farmhouses shaded by verandahs, cows and horses munching contentedly in meadows, venerable petrol stations, general stores advertising the untold delights of pies, pastries and cakes and, memorably, a sign saying, 'Poo. $2.50 a bag'. Bargain, if you ask me.

As dusk gathered us in and told us it was time to rest for the day, we found the sleepy port of Goolwa, which as I'm sure you know was voted South Australia's tidiest town in 2009, and if you didn't, they'll tell you with a large sign on the way in. A century and a half ago, we would have had trouble making our way down the main street through the raucous drunks spilling out from over one hundred inns and being carted off to the biggest police station in South Australia, for

Goolwa was a party town which was the last stop for the paddle steamers which made their way up and down the Murray River.

But then the railway came in 1852 and, almost overnight, the inns closed and the roar of laughter became the silence which we broke as we rode down the main street and almost ran over Robyn McColl from the local radio station as she ran into the street, sank to her knees and gave praise that something had happened in town for the first time since 1852.

Within half an hour we were booked to appear live on Alex FM in the morning, had checked into the Goolwa Central Motel, which was originally owned by an Irishman, dumped our bags in the Tyrone room, and were sitting in Murphy's Inn with a pint of Kilkenny in front of us and a Guinness and beef pie on the way. Nothing like travel to broaden your mind, I always say.

In the morning, we emerged from the studio after our live interview to greet our hordes of admiring listeners, but found only Paul, the manager of the Returned Services League, the Australian equivalent of the British Legion, opening up for business. Sighing deeply at our complete failure to achieve global superstardom, we rode east in glorious sunshine through the Barossa Valley, settled in the 1840s by Prussian Lutherans fleeing religious persecution and given sanctuary by South Australia, a state founded by the idealistic English entrepreneur Edward Wakefield as an antidote to the convict stain which he felt had befouled neighbouring New South Wales.

The Barossa Valley, of course, is today known much better for its fine vineyards, among which little stone Lutheran churches stand like nuns at an orgy, mute in perpetual disdain at the seeds of Bacchanalian debauchery which have been sown all around them. But then, when the Italians arrived in this part of the world and started planting their back gardens with fruit trees, vegetable patches and vineyards, the locals who had come from British stock mocked them as peasants, then sat down to tuck into meat stewed to death, vegetables boiled to buggery and tinned fruit with custard for afters.

By teatime we were in Meningie on the shore of Lake Albert, which merited precisely one line in the guidebook saying simply that there were places to stay. After exploring the highlights of the town, which took no time at all because there were none, we tracked down the Waterfront Motel.

Except that due to a combination of drought and silting, the waterfront itself had retreated to a quarter of a mile away, where it lay glittering in the setting sun, mocking a hotel jetty which reached out with as palpable and lost a yearning as the Lutheran spires down the road reached up to heaven above their empty pews.

I thought of my wife at home, half a world away, and decided it was probably time for a beer.

It was Matt's birthday and we had all been working pretty hard so at around 2 p.m. we decided to call it a day, catch up on some housekeeping, and celebrate. We seemed to be the only people at the motel, which used to have the freshwater Albert Lake – which is so big Geoff assumed it was the sea – lapping at its back door, but because of the Murray River dropping as water is diverted upstream, the edge of the water is now hundreds of yards away as the lake bed has dried out.

It's the big issue in town and the locals are up in arms, with a campaign underway to stop the damming. Motel owner Craig certainly didn't pull his punches when we spoke to him about it, 'They've stuffed it up for us down here good and proper, the bloody mongrels.'

That night I took Sam and Gloria outside onto the verandah to look at the velvety night sky and point out the Southern Cross. They were amazed that you could see the stars actually twinkle, something that has almost been lost in Europe, as light pollution spreads everywhere. Both said the whole trip was making them feel like kids again with each day bringing a new experience. As Sam put it, 'I still can't believe I'm here and this is all real.'

Thoughts echoed by all of us.

Our trusty and rusty backup, Matilda

4

In the morning, we did a bit of calculation and worked out that at our current rate of spending, we'd run out of money by the end of the week, and the entire trip would cost approximately £3.5 million. Even the fuel for Matilda would cost about £3,000, rather than the £3.56 we'd originally planned. Curses. If only I hadn't based the budget on John McDouall Stuart's epic 1858 expedition into the interior, which had cost £40 for food and £28 for his assistant's wages.

After some discussion, we decided that we had three options:

a) Get Gareth to stand on the roof of Matilda and lasso passing road trains, the huge trucks which thunder non-stop through the outback.

b) Blame each other for the worst piece of expedition planning since Scott and Co. set out for the South Pole.

c) Ignore the problem in the hope that it would go away.

Being blokes, we voted unanimously for 'c', then went for breakfast at the local bakery, which sported an impressive selection of pies – steak; steak and mushroom; steak and cheese; steak and onion; steak and bacon; steak, bacon and tomato; steak, bacon and cheese; steak and curry; steak and potato; steak and pepper; pizza pie; Hawaiian; chicken and vegetable (presumably for vegetarians); and a Ned Kelly. This turned out to be steak, egg and bacon – an Australian breakfast for men on the move. Behind the counter, meanwhile, were bottles of ginger beer and sarsaparilla.

We saved them for a lunch stop down the road and, as we sat on a weathered fence tucking into our pies and pop, an echelon of pelicans wheeled overhead, exquisite against the burning blue. Fifty yards down the road, however, was our first road kill of the trip – a young kangaroo lying in the verge.

'You won't get much sleep there, mate,' said Colin, polishing off the last of his Ned Kelly and hopping back on the bike.

About halfway to Kingston we stopped at a roadhouse for another drink and a break and as I sat outside in the shade, I was thrilled to see an old powder-blue Holden EJ station wagon pull into the forecourt, surfboards strapped to the roof. The old bus was almost completely original, right down to the venetian blinds in the back windows, and it was being driven by two young couples who were on a surfing safari all the way down the coast from Melbourne to Adelaide.

We stood and chatted for a bit while I admired their car, the same model that me and my mates had driven when we did exactly the same thing almost thirty years before. I was pleased that the tradition of heading off down the coast, just following the surf, still continued.

We pressed on towards Kingston, and with no time pressure – we had a date with a music festival in Victoria in four days and plenty of time to get there – we just enjoyed the ride.

Rosie and I were really bonding now and I was starting to feel at home with her, getting used to her personality. Every bike, even of the same model, feels different and has its own unique charateristics. I'd now reached the stage where if you put me on Geoff's bike blindfolded, I'd know it wasn't mine. Rosie was singing along, my new Triumph boots and riding gear were starting to loosen up and feel comfortable, the sun was shining and the road was perfect. I couldn't wait until we got out on the really long stretches so I could see exactly what the bike could do.

We got our first glimpse of the Southern Ocean as we rode into Kingston. The town was smaller than we'd thought, with only two main commercial streets and everything else running off them, but it was bright and tidy and seemingly on the up, as there was quite a bit of building and regeneration going on.

At the end of the main street, the blue ocean stretched off into the empty distance until it reached the slightly lighter blue sky, where there was nothing until you reached Antarctica.

Kingston's highlights included a tractor museum, a giant lobster to celebrate the main industry, and a hotel that would not be featuring in the *Michelin Guide*, this year or any other. We dumped our bags in a room whose air conditioning took the form of a broken window, and went downstairs for the $10 fish and chips special.

'No worries, mate. You want your fish grilled, crumbed or battered?'

'You spoil me. Crumbed, and two pints of Coopers' Pale while you're at it,' I said.

'That's not a pint,' said Colin when I brought the beer down to the table.

'Yes it is. I've just ordered it.'

'No it's not, mate. It's only called a pint in South Australia, but it's less than an imperial pint. In Victoria it's called a pot, in New South Wales and Western Oz it's a middie, in the Northern Territory it's a handle, and in Queensland it's a schooner. Except don't ask for a schooner in South Australia, or you'll get half a pint, which in all the other states is called a glass. Unless it's a pony, which is even smaller.'

Well, thank heavens to get that sorted out, I thought, taking a long cold swallow and deciding that after a long, hot day on the road battling giant crayfish and dead kangaroos, it was delicious whatever it was called.

In the morning, I wandered down to the general store and asked the cheery teenager behind the counter if he had any butter.

'You what, mate?' he said.

'Butter. You know, for spreading on toast.'

'Oh, you mean *bata*.'

I should hardly have been surprised. Australians have long ditched the r as an imperial frippery, so that Cairns becomes *Cens*, water *wata* and that thing you drive around, a *ca*.

That afternoon, we rolled into the idyllic seaside village of Robe, all sandstone and roses around the doors, found a motel with wi-fi, and sat down to file our weekly stories and pictures to the *Daily Mirror* and the Triumph and Adelaide Adventures websites. I had just logged on when Colin emerged from the bathroom.

'Here, mate, what time is it?'

'Time you got a watch, you Aussie drongo.'

'Nah, never wear one, mate.'

'Why don't you check on your mobile phone?'

'Haven't had one since I hurled it at the kitchen wall.'

'Ah yes, I forgot. It's ten to –'

'Beaut. Think I'll go for a swim then come back and watch the footie.'

'No worries. Just give me the memory stick with your stuff for the *Mirror* and websites.'

'Oh yeah. Is that today? What time is it again?'

'Nearly two.'

'Well, I'm starving, so I'll go out and get a pie, then come back and write the stuff while I watch the footie,' he said, disappearing out the door. Half an hour later, he came back with a pie, switched on the TV and hauled out his laptop.

'Bloody hell, can't get the adaptor into the power socket,' he said.

'Well, just run it on the battery.'

'Can't, mate. The battery's buggered.'

'Well, why didn't you buy a new one before you left home, you dickhead?'

'No need. I never use the bloody thing,' he said, wandering next door to get another adaptor from the film crew. He came back, plugged it in, and sat down.

'Here, mate, how do you get an internet connection?'

'I just gave you the access code. What's the problem?'

'Dunno, mate.'

'Here, let's have a look. Bloody hell, the screen's practically black. Where's the brightness control?'

'No point, mate. Bloody thing's knackered.'

His life was only saved at this point when we remembered that the two surfer dudes driving that ancient Holden station wagon the day before had told us that on Wednesday the Robe Bowling Club had an open bowling and barbie evening.

Two hours later, having finally filed all our stories and pictures, we were being introduced to the joys of lawn bowling by Bet Allsop, the feisty seventy-eight-year-old former club president who was typical of a country in which pensioners are supercharged rather than superannuated. Several of the owners of guest houses we had stayed in already, for example, were in their eighties and still going strong.

'You on the bikes I saw earlier?' said Bet by way of introduction. 'I had a lovely AJS 350 with telescopic front forks and a rigid back end, then I got married at twenty-three and pregnant at twenty-five, so that was the end of that. Right, lads, off you go, and for God's sake call them bowls, not balls, although I won't go into the reason why, since this is a family club,' she said, ushering us out onto an immaculate green on which the only sounds were couples walking their dogs on the beach below and the occasional kiss of bowl on jack, followed by cries of 'Lovely shot, Bruce' and a gentle tsunami of applause.

As Bet led Geoff and I down the green, she looked around and admonished, 'Bring your beer with you!'

'I could get to like this game,' I thought. The crack was ninety as, indeed, were several of the participants, and we had a great time watching them skipping around, perhaps not quite like teenagers, but certainly not like pensioners. There was slagging galore going on and we also noticed a few Vietnam veteran badges among the old boys, a reminder of Australia's hefty involvement in that conflict.

Despite Bet's best attempts at coaching us, Gloria, Sam and I were thrashed 17–5 by Geoff, Matt and Gareth, but then Geoff revealed that he had been hiding his bowls under a bushel so to speak, and that as a teenager he had been a county indoor champion. I told the locals and their verdict was, 'Let's take him round the back and kick him in the nuts,' so we claimed the moral victory.

Of course, I had merely thought it would be immodest of me to mention that at the age of sixteen I had been a county triples bowling champion until I'd had to give it up to do my O Levels. Bet, meanwhile, was handing over the prize for the best score of the evening to the visiting team from Ridge River, who were in town for the main competition the next day, and who had been preparing for it by drinking steadily since breakfast. Rather sportingly, they then handed the prize money back to a grateful Bet.

'Thanks, lads. That's the easiest $40 I've made in a night for a long time,' she said.

We gave Bet a big hug before we left, and gave her another one when we saw her the next morning as we were dandering around the village before packing up and heading on.

'Bet, we were dreaming of you all night,' I said.

'No wonder I couldn't sleep,' she beamed, then gave us another hug for good measure.

Back at the motel, we packed up and were ready to go when I

suddenly realised I'd lost the bike key. I searched in every bag I had, then the room and everywhere else, followed by the handbags of several passing women and under the motel cat, then finally found it exactly where I'd left it.

I started the bike, then wondered if I'd put my wallet in the inside pocket of my jacket, and checked that. Then I had to check that my glasses were in the other pocket, my notebook was in the tank bag and my feet were attached to the ends of my legs.

'For God's sake, man, stop farting about,' said Colin, who seemed to have completely forgotten his epic farting about performance the day before.

'It's not farting about. As I explained to Clifford Paterson when we rode from Chile to Alaska, it's poggling, which is a whole different kettle of ball games,' I said. 'In the same way that Samurai warriors used to meditate before they went into battle to make sure that their action arose out of the purity of stillness, my action of riding off down the road is preceded by a period of mindless activity called poggling to help me connect with the nothingness at the centre of my being.'

'Nothingness at the centre of your head, more like,' he said, roaring off then stalling, giving me that rare Greco-German pleasure of *Schadenfreude* resulting from hubris.

Sadly, I was to suffer the same myself five minutes later with the first equipment failure of the trip when the snazzy sliding sun visor on my helmet became detached. Still, nothing that a spot of superglue didn't sort out, for which I'd just like to thank the entire staff of two in Thrifty Link Hardware of Millicent, where we stopped for a Magnum bar, it being hotter than July in Hell that day.

As a piece of innovation, it was hardly up there with the unflappable Alfred Howitt, who set out from Melbourne in July 1861 to search for the remains of the ill-fated Burke and Wills expedition during which they had attempted to cross the continent from south to north. Discovering that both had perished, Howitt hauled out a carrier pigeon to send the news back, only to find that the willow basket had worn away the unfortunate bird's tail feathers. Undeterred, he shot a wild pigeon, spliced its feathers onto the carrier pigeon with cobblers' wax, and after a quick test flight around his tent, sent the bird on its way.

Helmet fixed, I rode on, then realised I was getting high on superglue fumes, so I opened the visor a smidgen as we rode through a landscape which changed suddenly from sun-baked meadows to glades of aromatic pine, so that you expected at any moment to see handmaidens dancing naked through the trees singing old Swedish folk songs. Sadly, no maidens appeared, so they were obviously on their tea break, sipping elderflower cordial from sun-dappled buttercups.

By our own teatime, we were at Mount Gambier, a pleasant town with its head resting on the wooded slopes of a hopefully extinct volcano, and its toes cooling in an azure lake.

We found a motel with wi-fi and I was able to check my e-mail. Even better, I discovered that the handlebars of the Tiger made a perfect place for drying your socks and, with a sense of accomplishment I wandered into town with Colin for a beer without a single bit of poggling, since the thought of a beer creates its own pure stillness, followed immediately on application by the feeling of contentment which Australians describe wonderfully as the warm fuzzies.

On the way back, we picked up some pizza, that well-known Oz speciality, and arrived at the motel room to find Matt and Gareth just back from filming at the lake. Before long, Colin was blogging, Matt was uploading, Gareth was downloading and I was reading *The Explorers* by Tim Flannery. Chuck Berry was on the radio and cricket was on the TV.

It was either a seething crucible of digital innovation, or a microcosm of the lunatic complexity of modern life, but either way, global media domination could only be hours away.

'Here, guys, should I be worried that I was humming "Puppy Love" inside my helmet this afternoon?' I said at one stage.

'Deeply,' said Gareth.

'There's obviously some wiring loose in your internal iPod,' said Matt. 'From now on, I want regular reports on your tune for the day.'

At last we tumbled into our various beds, and I was woken at dawn by the sweet warbling of two magpies outside the window. Like R2D2 after a spliff, their song was utterly different to the call of their cousins at home, who sound more like a fight in cutlery drawer. The lads got up to rustle up some breakfast, Gareth stuck the Beach Boys on his iPod, and all was well with the world.

As for me, I couldn't suppress my excitement as this was the day we were heading to my home state of Victoria, and the world-famous four-day Port Fairy Folk Festival. Port Fairy was once known as Belfast, as it was settled by people from the north of Ireland, particularly County Antrim, and it still retains a distinct Irish flavour. The town was then renamed to what some say is a corruption of Portaferry in County Down. For years the council area was still known as the Shire of Belfast, until it was again renamed after the River Moyne which runs through the town, meaning it is now known as Moyne Council, again like the north Antrim version, so in a way it has come full circle.

Back in the early 1800s an Irish family called Henty had settled here looking for freedom from authority and a place of their own. They sailed across from Tasmania without telling anyone, brought their livestock and set up a homestead. Around twenty years later, when the explorer Thomas Mitchell came over a rise in what he thought was virgin territory, he found cattle ranging across the horizon and a substantial settlement built up.

More Irish followed the Hentys until the whole region developed a peculiarly Irish character, with towns called Killarney, Coleraine and of course Belfast/Port Fairy. At many shops and outlets along the road I noticed the Irish tricolour flying alongside the Aussie flag, an indication of how proud the people are of their Irish heritage.

I'd been to this festival many times before over the years, but it had grown exponentially since then and I was looking forward to seeing it all again – plus one of my best mates, Kevin Rafferty, a total music-head, photographer and all-round good egg, would be there to greet us, though I knew he was a bit miffed that we'd blagged media passes to all areas, while he, who'd never missed a festival since the 1980s, had to pay – bloody foreigners!

The festival was reputed to be so popular that the tourist board had told us we hadn't a chance of finding a room within several thousand miles of the place. Naturally, after a quick phone call that morning, we found somewhere in Warrnambool, fifteen minutes away.

Rather than head straight to the hotel, we decided to set off for Port Fairy itself. Half an hour down the road, we crossed the state border into Victoria, and almost immediately the landscape changed from rolling downs, to meadows and stands of Norfolk pine.

It was just like home, except for the fact that the meadows were the size of Wales, and it became even more like home when a rare cloud appeared in the sky, followed by all his mates, who then came down for a closer look. As we slogged east it began to rain and, at one stage, I dimly glimpsed the propellers of a wind farm turning in the gathering murk, like the giant gravestones of pilots who had been lost in cloud.

Naturally, since I had failed yet again to remember to put my trousers outside my boots, they soon had an inch of water sloshing around in the bottom. And so, having left Belfast in a downpour a week before, we arrived in the town formerly known as Belfast in much the same, to find that it was the first time it had rained on this weekend for sixteen years.

Still, it seemed appropriate for a folk festival, I thought as I squelched down the main street past rose-draped picket fences, feeling like an extra in *It's a Wonderful Life*, and into a vast meadow which housed entire families of giant marquees, like a

Bedouin metropolis. Naturally, I was immediately accosted by a pair of street performers, a Scotsman on stilts whose fake wolfhound greeted me warmly then peed on my foot.

We made our way to the organiser's tent where the friendly bohemian staff gave us our 'access all areas' press passes. In reality these were little more than wristbands with 'performer' on them but they pleased Geoff and myself no end, given our desire for mass public adulation and global media domination.

I was amazed at the change in the town. Once a sleepy hollow and almost on the verge of becoming a ghost town, it appears to have boomed over the past two decades. When I was last here, some twenty years ago, many of the shops in the main streets were closed, and countless houses stood empty with forlorn 'For Sale' signs tacked on to their peeling paintwork.

It's quite a different story today, and the secret of Port Fairy is out, largely because of the festival, which is now a must-do on the list of performers, from folkies, to roots and blues, country and western and anything in between. The Monks of Tibet were even there this year. What's next, The Three Priests? Or maybe the people of Port Fairy have suffered enough.

Our performer passes worked a treat and we hobnobbed it in the green room with the acts, eating pies and drinking beer – sophisticated hangers on that we were. In between, we wandered around the festival arena, taking it all in. There were all kinds of food and music stalls, clothes and art booths and just about every 'groovy' kind of goods you could think of, while kids were catered for by comedic magicians and clowns.

We made our way to the main arena where Colin Hay, formerly of the band Men at Work, was performing live. The arena itself was huge – it must have held upwards of five thousand people under a circus-style, big-top marquee – and I was again amazed at the way the festival has grown. Performing in front of such a huge crowd didn't seem to faze

Colin though, and he put on a great show. He's a class act and he filled the gaps between numbers with various stories about his life, both amusing and poignant.

As writer of the band's biggest hit, 'Down Under', Colin had been involved in a recent court case in which it was claimed that the well-known flute riff from the song had actually been appropriated from another Australian classic, 'Kookabura'. It was clearly a sensitive subject, but Colin kept a running joke going about it, introducing many of his numbers by saying, 'Here's another one I stole.' The crowd laughed along with him, and gave him a standing ovation when the set was over.

I struck lucky afterwards and met him while he sat outside signing copies of his CDs. I seized my chance and asked if we could perhaps have a chat on camera the next day. He agreed and we parted ways with the usual, 'My people will contact your people' line – ah, the heady whiff of celebrity.

However, hearing Colin play live wasn't the best part of the evening, though his song about a man who went into a shop every day because he fancied the girl behind the counter and was too shy to tell her was just wonderful. 'There's more than one Uncle Fred in the world,' I thought as I sat and listened to the sacred silence between his words. No, the best part was the fact that, for the entire hour he was on stage, a fly buzzed around in the spotlight, captured for posterity on the three giant TV screens around the auditorium and thinking all the while: 'Wow, look at all those people who've come to see little me! Me, Frank the Fly! Is my hair all right? Is my fly open? Oh wait, I am a fly. Is my man open?'

The show ended, Colin left the stage to rapturous applause after an encore of 'Down Under', and Frank flew home at lightning speed to break the news to Mrs Frank and the little Franks.

As we rode home ourselves, we passed a large sign in a field saying: 'Farm for sale by expression of interest'. What did that mean? That someone who phoned up and said they were *really* interested would get it over someone who was only slightly interested? Almost certainly, one would hope.

Standing out on the verandah of the motel the next morning I reflected that it was the little things about being home that struck me – like how the wooden posts holding up the roof don't go all the way to the ground but have about three inches of steel bar going into the concrete. To stop termites eating the wood, I remembered. Funny thing, the old memory.

Feeling nostalgic, and more than a little glad to be back, I decided to head off early and take the bike down to Port Fairy again. I loved the freedom of the road and the flexibility of having Rosie nearby – I was starting to feel naked without her around. Maybe there is something in Flann O'Brien's theory that all men are part bicycle.

Traffic heading to the festival was manic though. At least it was for this part of the world anyway, I must have passed at least a dozen cars on the way – total gridlock, man.

As I rode back to Port Fairy the next morning for the second day of the festival, it seemed as if half of Victoria was out playing tennis, skateboarding, cycling or running, and the other half was sailing or surfing.

Much of the Aussie's love of sport is the result of the climate, which in Ireland encourages you to go out and hit someone, but in Australia encourages you to go out and hit a ball, but it is also the result of the Montreal Olympics in 1976, when Australia came home with a paltry silver and four bronzes, said 'Stuff that, mate' and poured billions into sports development, giving a nation of only twenty million people 14 golds, 15 silvers and 17 bronze medals at the 2008 Olympics in Beijing, not to mention world titles in more sports than you can swing a racquet at.

Colin had gone to the festival a little early in an effort to find his friend Kevin, who he claimed had come down from Melbourne.

'Can't miss him, mate. Walks with a stick, looks like Ned Kelly, drives a vintage gold Ford Fairlane,' he had said the evening before, then completely failed to find him in spite of exploring the entire town and making several calls on my mobile, leaving me increasingly convinced that Kevin was in fact Colin's imaginary friend. 'You wouldn't catch me getting involved in that kind of thing,' I remember saying to Jim the rabbit.

The day was spent wandering around in a happy daze, popping into marquees just because you liked the sound coming from them, wondering how women could wear so little and not be arrested, and trying on Tibetan hats and rainbow pullovers.

The highlight of the day for me was meeting up with Colin Hay again, who graciously allowed us to film him at his CD signing before giving us an interview, which was more like a chat with a bloke you just met in the pub. He also graciously allowed us to give him $30 for his latest CD. Still, I guess he needs the cash after what that flaming 'Kookaburra' song did to him.

We chatted for a while and discussed our shared backgrounds as Ten Pound Tourists. Colin had come over on the boat from Scotland with his family in 1967, and he too had experienced feelings of alienation and awe at being dropped into such a strange new country. Many of his songs reflect this, and the sense of belonging to and loving two places at the same time. It's ironic that he, as an immigrant, went on to write such an anthem as 'Down Under', which is recognised the world over as quintessentially Australian. Perhaps sometimes it takes a sense of being an outsider to so keenly observe a country and society. We swapped a bit of banter about the experience of being dropped into this huge barren land, which has so much in it – and joked about the fact that unfortunately most of it is trying to kill you.

Sadly our time to talk was soon over but he told us to stay in touch through his website, so we told him to piss off, that he could stay in touch on ours. He's a great guy and a fantastic songwriter and performer – just don't mention kookaburras!

 We rode back to Warrnambool and went out for a takeaway pizza from a local restaurant, narrowly avoiding being kidnapped and raped by a hen party.

'Here, you're really tall. Are you tall all over?' said one of them, a slim brunette called Cheryl.

'Nah, hung like a gerbil,' I said.

'Don't believe ya,' she grinned as our pizzas arrived and saved our virginities just in time.

'Tune for the day?' said Matt as we arrived back with the nosh.

'"Itchycoo Park",' I said. 'Was that by The Small Faces?'

'Much better,' said Matt as Gareth handed out the pizzas.

Cruising along on the Great Ocean Road

5

The next morning we took a quick spin around Warrnambool and stopped at Logan's Beach, a place which had been the scene of many of my teenage surfing adventures. The beach is just as magnificent now as it was then and there were plenty of surfers there for us to watch.

Warrnambool was once a whaling centre, as just off the coast is a major whale migratory route for the Southern Right Whale. It was so-named by the whalers because it was the 'right' type of whale to harpoon as it gives so much oil and, as a result, they were hunted and slaughtered to the brink of extinction. Now that whaling has ceased – apart from our Nipponese cousins and their spurious scientific killing expeditions – the Southern Rights are back, and the cliffs outside Warrnambool have become a haven for whale watchers, instead of a lookout for harpooners.

The giant creatures, which can reach up to sixteen metres in length, pass as close as a few hundred yards from shore, and in the crystal water you can see them clearly. Sometimes a mother and calf will come right into the bay to shelter and put on a performance that will bring people flocking from miles around.

Then it was time for the Great Ocean Road, which begins just outside the town of Port Campbell. The area has fantastic sweeping vistas of cliffs and ocean, and we were quite looking forward to that stretch of the journey. All we had to do to stay on course was to keep the sea on our right – which thankfully even we could manage. Though we still had to keep an eye on Geoff as he had trouble with the concept of left and right. I warned him, 'cliffs, sudden death and sharks on the right; poisonous snakes, spiders, lethal kangaroos, dingoes and, of course, the killer wombats, on the left' just to give him some focus.

 The Great Ocean Road is one of the wonders of the world – apart from the Magnum ice-cream bar and beer. Stretching for one hundred and seventy six miles, it was built between 1919 and 1932 to commemorate the Australian soldiers who died in the First World War, to give employment to those who returned, and to rival Pacific Coast Highway in California as one of the planet's great scenic drives.

We stopped at London Bridge, a double-arched rock formation whose outer span collapsed in 1990, stranding a couple on the other side so that they had to be rescued by helicopter. Sadly, they turned out to be having an affair, and got a bit of a shock when they landed to find several TV crews waiting to hear the story of their thrilling rescue. And an even bigger shock when they got home to be greeted by a frying pan, I imagine.

However, since the chances of Colin and I having an affair were approximately the same as either of us winning the lottery, we were free to enjoy the view, which in both directions as far as the eye could see consisted of sandstone cliffs worn by wind and waves into fantastical shapes which in places resembled eyes and ears, noses and mouths, so that you imagined an entire coastline composed of mythical beings, sleeping by the sea until the day when they awake and surprise us all.

I was obviously hallucinating due to a shortage of beer, so we rode the short distance down the coast to Port Campbell and parked in front of the only hotel just as the rain started again.

'Used to work here on my summer holidays. I'll nip in and see if my mates who run the place are still here,' said Colin, getting off his bike and walking inside, only to reappear two minutes later.' Nah, they've gone to Bali,' he said.

'What, with Kevin?' I said, beginning to suspect that all Colin's friends were imaginary. Checking in the nearest mirror to make sure I was real, I had a pint of local ale and an early supper, and went to bed, drained by the heat and the humidity, as outside the raindrops pattered on the verandah and lightning split the sky.

Next morning, the chaps discovered that the hotel had a washing machine and dumped a week's worth of laundry into it only to discover, when sorting the Adelaide team shirts out afterwards, that the results of their vigorous enjoyment of Antipodean cuisine had beaten even the industrial might of Bosch.

'Here, Colin, this is definitely yours. I remember that pizza stain from last Wednesday.'

'Nah, mate, mine's the one with the pie mark from Tuesday. Look, there it is.'

Being a more fastidious adventurer who handwashed his shirt and socks every night, I left them to it and wandered down the main street to get some bread and marmalade for brekkie, passing surf shops and little cafés filled with people who were, almost without exception, gorgeous.

But then, it was hardly surprising: in the eighteenth and nineteenth centuries, when the poor in England were being hanged for stealing a currant bun or looking sideways at a sheep, judges often took pity on the young and beautiful and sent them to a thrilling new life in Botany Bay instead.

The same thing happened after the Second World War, when Australia realised that it needed to populate or perish, but immigration officials, all too aware of the dregs of racism left over from the official White Australia policy of the 1920s, only picked the best looking of the assorted applicants to make them more acceptable to the predominantly Anglo-Saxon population.

As Minister for Immigration Arthur Calwell put it when recommending that Australia turn to 'the beautiful Balts' rather than southern Europe for the first wave of post-war immigrants: 'Many were red-headed and blue-eyed. There were also a number of natural platinum blondes of both sexes. The men were handsome and the women beautiful. It was not hard to sell immigration to the Australian people once the press published photographs of that group.'

Even when the country did begin admitting Italian, Greek, Slav and Jewish refugees, Jews were limited to three thousand per year, and officials were careful to pick only the more light-skinned of applicants. It was, ironically, an Aussie version of the Nazi Aryan policies which those refugees were fleeing in the first place.

'Sorry, mate, you're too swarthy. Next!'

Even if migrants did get in, they were forced to work at whatever the government decided for the first two years. As Phillip Knightley pointed out in his book *Australia: A Biography of a Nation*, this led to doctors, dentists, musicians and teachers toiling away in road gangs, canning factories or building projects such as the huge Snowy Mountains Scheme, on which an Australian surgeon was performing a tracheotomy one day, watched by a Czech ambulance driver. As the surgeon was just about to make the first incision, the driver yelled, 'No! Not there! Cut here!'

'Listen, mate, I happen to be following the instructions of a world authority on this procedure,' said the surgeon, waving a manual.

'Yes, yes, but there have been developments since I wrote that,' said the driver.

Oh, and Australians really do call each other mate. All the time. As Robert Hughes said in *The Fatal Shore*, the great

Australian concept of mateship probably emerged from the need for convicts to help each other or die. Once those convicts had served their time they often became shepherds or cattlemen, forced to make a hard and lonely living in the bush, and as Alexander Harris said in *Settlers and Convicts*: 'Men under these circumstances often stand by one another through thick and thin; in fact, it is a universal feeling that a man ought to be able to trust his mate in anything.'

It made Australia utterly different not only from the Britain from which they came, but from the USA which, as Andreas Whittam Smith has pointed out, was also a British colony, also English-speaking, and also faced initially friendly then hostile indigenous people, yet developed a completely different ethos of every man for himself and the devil take the hindmost.

And it was a principle that was hardened rather than melted in the fiercest crucible of all: war. As Gavan Dawes wrote in *Prisoners of the Japanese*, during the Second World War the British POWs hung onto their class structure to the point of death and the Americans turned into capitalist gangsters who charged interest on borrowed rice, but the Australians created a series of tiny welfare states in which they shared everything with their mates.

When the Japanese freighter *Rokyu Maru*, with 599 British and 649 Australian prisoners of war on board, was torpedoed by American submarines in 1944, a group of English survivors who had been drifting for days spotted a huge group of rafts carefully tied together. As they got closer, they recognised the familiar slouch hats of the Aussies, and a rope was tossed across to them, followed by a friendly voice saying, 'Cheers, mate. This is no place to be on your lonesome.'

Intriguingly, that sense of cooperation can even be found in flora and fauna: according to Phillip Knightley, plants in Australia live in a symbiotic relationship in which they recycle nutrients for each other; and young male kookaburras who are old enough to leave the nest will hang around, helping their parents incubate eggs then food for their little brothers and sisters, often foregoing forever their own chances of finding a mate and setting up home.

Sadly though, while it may include the wildlife, mateship doesn't extend to women: as Knightley points out, one of the most telling things you can do at an Aussie dinner party is to ask all the women at the table who their best mates are. They will invariably name their husbands. Then ask the men, and watch the expression on the faces of the women as their husbands name someone they were at school with, their golfing partner, or someone they go fishing with.

There. Having sorted that out, I returned from the general store to find my socks and shirt drying nicely on the bike's handlebars. Making a mental note to write to Mr Triumph congratulating him on making a machine with such a variety of uses, I tore the note up, threw it in a bin which didn't exist, and got the toast and coffee organised for my mates.

Once they'd finished that we set off for the Twelve Apostles, a row of naturally formed two-hundred-foot-high limestone stacks off the coast, named after the disciples of an obscure Middle Eastern religious sect called Christianity which got as far as Northern Ireland then died out, not through lack of interest, but through too much.

Sadly, we'd spent so much time farting about with laundry that by the time we got there, there were only half a dozen of the Apostles left. Thankfully, though, it turned out not to have been our fault, or even cutbacks caused by the recession, but simply by the erosion which had separated them from the original coastline in the first place.

 The guys were stunned at the spectacle, as was I, despite having been here many times in the past. In fact, I'd been coming here back when there were at least eleven of the Apostles left. The drop in number was not the only change to this natural wonder however – now there were hordes of people streaming back and forward along the new tunnel which runs under the road from the new visitor centre onto purpose-built viewing platforms. Helicopters constantly circled overhead giving people a bird's eye view of the ocean and the limestone pillars which are sadly disappearing as the coast erodes them by around two centimetres per year. They are an icon for this part of the coast and were more than worth seeing again.

We rode off around a bluff, followed by Matt and Gareth in Matilda, only to come upon an astonishing sight: thousands of tiny birds like starlings nestling in hollows along the cliff, turning it almost completely black. We stopped, and Matt came over.

'Listen, this is going to be the greatest shot of all time if we can get them flying off the cliff face en masse. We just have to be dead quiet so we don't disturb them,' he said.

We freewheeled down the hill with the engines off to the best viewpoint, and Matt tiptoed around to the side door of the van to get out the camera, but just as he was setting it up, a gust of wind slammed the door shut, and the entire flock of birds rose as one and disappeared from sight, leaving him with the greatest shot never taken. On the other side of the planet, David Attenborough rolled over and went back to sleep, his reputation safe for another week or so.

As for us, we packed up and drove on through the Otway Hills, a modest name for a stunning landscape of alpine woods and meadows dotted with quaint wooden farmhouses, so that I expected at any minute to see Julie Andrews come skipping gaily down a grassy slope singing selected hits from *The Sound of Music*, only to trip on an edelweiss and go arse over tit in a flurry of freshly laundered petticoats.

If the landscape was Swiss, though, the weather was pure Irish: gale-force winds interspersed with horizontal downpours. We gritted our teeth and rode on, at one stage passing a row of side roads with Lithuanian names – Kaunaskis and the like – at another, meeting a family touring in the American fashion, in a camper van the size of a Greyhound bus towing a double-decker trailer loaded with a Jeep, a boat and two motorbikes, and at another still, emerging from a long run of forest to see on our left a symphony of hills and dales straight out of Middle Earth, with the ocean beyond.

As you can imagine, after such a Tolkeinesque Swiss-American-Lithuanian-Irish experience, it was in a state of some cultural confusion that we descended at last to the beachfront village of Apollo Bay to find that Colin actually had some real friends: Toj and Jo, who lived in the woods overlooking the bay.

Since creatures are always attracted to their emotional and intellectual equals, I was immediately adopted by their golden greyhound Ray, who leaned against my left leg, and by Tiger their chocolatey Burmese, who wrapped herself around my right ankle with a brief introductory purr followed by an earshattering 'Mwaooooh!' which translated from Cat meant: 'I love you. Now feed me or die, earthling.'

Joanna and Toj lived just outside the town in a little hamlet called Skene's Creek, having moved there from Melbourne to escape the city and to take life a little easier. Jo and I had gone to high school together, and she is one of my oldest friends, while she and Toj had been together for close to thirty years.

After our heartfelt reunion, we all piled into Matilda and headed out for dinner where the crack was great and Jo, Toj and I were able to catch up on the past few years, remembering many of the more embarrassing episodes of our wild youth. Toj was a motor mechanic and had run a garage with his two brothers after they took over from their dad, but he had decided to retire early. Jo then quit her job and together they moved down to the surf coast where he does the odd bit of mechanical work, fixes up the house and goes fishing, while Jo makes clothes to sell at the country market, giving herself some extra income. It's an idyllic lifestyle that many would envy.

The next day we awoke to a chorus of kookaburras in the gum trees around the house. It would be our last stretch of the Great Ocean Road and, for me, potentially the most thrilling part of the ride, as well as being a blast from my past. As we carved our way around cliff faces and hairpins, down into valleys and up mountains, all the while with the raging surf on our right, it was like a roadmap of my youth – the names of the beaches and towns brought back so many vivid memories for me.

Apollo Bay, where one of mates' family had a holiday house; Kennet River, where we used to camp; Wye River, where another mate had a house; Lorne, where the pub is mad, in the summer; Angelsea, which has some great surf breaks and a stunning view as you drive in; Torquay, where I first learned to surf and fell in love with the whole scene; and Jan Juc, my favourite beach of all time where I caught my first 'tube' – getting right inside the curl of the wave for the very first time. This had been my weekend and holiday playground and it was as gorgeous as ever, even if it was now teeming with people compared to when I first discovered it.

Around halfway to Torquay, where we had planned to take a break, we saw our first koala – a big male who was sitting on a branch that hung right out over the road around twenty feet from the ground. He was taking absolutely no notice of the people underneath him taking pictures, and simply hung there half-asleep.

We stopped at Point Addis where I used to fish off the cliff. The point is now fenced off and designated wooden walkways have been constructed to protect the area but, while I appreciated the motives, I couldn't help but feel sad that another part of my youth, and the freedom I had back then was now gone – now no one would ever know the thrill of fishing into the wild surf from the point as we once had. I wasn't the first to fish from there though, not by a long chalk, and I took a little comfort in that.

*

One of the more famous people who was known to have fished from this point was William Buckley, a remarkable convict known as 'The Wild White Man'. In 1803, and aged just twenty-three, Buckley had been transported from England to a settlement at Sorrento on the shore of Port Phillip Bay. He escaped and for the next thirty-two years lived with the local Watourong tribe, hunting and fishing alongside them at places like Godocut, the Koorie name for Point Addis. He was initiated into many of the tribe's rites and became a senior member, with some believing that he fathered many children.

Buckley finally left the tribe when other white settlers arrived in the locality, appearing out of the virgin bush to their complete amazement. At first he had forgotten his own language but was identified as an escaped convict by a tattoo on his arm. He became an instant celebrity. He was pardoned and managed to secure employment as an interpreter for John Batman – the man credited with founding Melbourne – before marrying and moving to Tasmania, where he held a minor government position until he died in 1856, aged seventy-six. His story had always fascinated me and, as I stood on that cliff top, I once again imagined him and his Koorie companions living in and moving about the region, and the travails and perils they must have faced.

Wild, iconoclastic men of speed

6

From Torquay it was a straight run into Melbourne and thankfully the weather held, as I had a little treat for my travelling companions – I had made sure that our journey would take us into Melbourne via the Westgate Freeway and over the Westgate Bridge – one of the most dramatic road entrances into a city in the world. The Westgate spans the River Yarra estuary and is the longest and highest bridge in the southern hemisphere – as you climb up it from the west, the skyscrapers of the city appear on your left and the bay, dotted with sails, is on your right. It's certainly got the 'wow' factor, and everyone was suitably impressed.

For my part, I was excited to be home and was looking forward to seeing my sister Liese, her family and all my old mates. Liese is the only one out of the six of us still currently living in Australia, the rest of us having left to wander the globe, though I suspect that one day most of us will move back to 'the lucky country'. She and her husband Brad had known about our trip, but we had been so busy organising it that I had not told them exactly when I would be there, so I knew my visit would come as a surprise.

Sam and Gloria would be leaving us here, so we all decided

to go out for dinner. I booked us into the restaurant that Brad runs – just to prove to the team that I also had relatives as well as friends – and his jaw fell open when I walked in. I couldn't have asked for a better reaction.

Despite the surprise, he made us all welcome, and we had a fabulous 'last supper' together as the dirty half-dozen. We all had a bit to drink and the farewells were effusive, but heartfelt, as we had all grown close to Sam and Gloria, who had become an intrinsic part of the team.

 What Colin neglects to mention, of course, was his epic bout of poggling as we rode into Melbourne, a city of sun-dappled boulevards and tram bells, shady parks and sailboats in the bay, and Victorian gold rush mansions reflected in glass skyscrapers.

'Will we just follow Matilda to the hotel, since the lads have it programmed into Nichola?' I said as we filled up at a petrol station on the way in.

'No need, mate. I grew up in this town,' said Colin, then promptly got us lost.

'Didn't have all these one-way systems when I grew up here,' he said by way of explanation as we arrived at the hotel a good half hour after Matilda.

However, I got my revenge in the Poggle Wars when I left the keys in the bike ignition for two hours outside the hotel the next morning. Whatever you do, don't tell the folks at Triumph.

My only excuse was that I was suffering from whiplash of the liver from the farewell bash to Sam and Gloria the night before, and I was still not a well man as we went walking around the city which, as Colin has mentioned, could easily have been named after John Batman, the early settler who walked over yon far eastern hill and said: 'I say, that looks like a nice spot for a town', but the honour fell instead to Lord Henry William Melbourne, and poor old John's legacy lingers only in assorted Batman Parks and Streets.

Geoff may have been feeling the effects of the night before, but I was full of energy and took great pride in showing the boys around 'my town'. They made all the right noises – partly, I suspect, out of good manners, or perhaps fear that I'd release some noxious local nasty in their beds – and as I looked out at the familiar sights it seemed as though I had never been away.

We did a walking tour of the city centre, and I brought the guys to see the huge Victoria Market which had been a life-saver when I was a student, as we bought all our meat and fruit and veg there. We used go down on a Saturday and wait until the market was about to close, as then the various butchers and fishmongers would stage an impromptu auction to get rid of the rest of their stock – as a result we were often able to get a tray of steak for just a few dollars. Fruit and veg were always pretty cheap if you bought in season, and for penniless students, we lived pretty well.

After the market, I took everyone to see the remains of the Old Melbourne Gaol. Only part of the original structure remains as the rest of the site was taken up by RMIT University – which took over some of the buildings and used rubble from the others for new blocks – but it is still a fascinating place to visit. The gaol was built out of a local granite known as bluestone, so inmates there were often described as having gone to 'bluestone college'. With RMIT being my former university, I'm quite proud of the fact that I can claim to have gone to bluestone college myself without having been locked up for twenty-three hours a day – though some of my former tutors might have thought that this was not a bad idea.

The gaol stands as a glum shrine to the nineteenth-century Pentonville system – a method of prison management named after the eponymous prison in London, in which prisoners were incarcerated for up to twenty-three hours a day, in a silence broken only by the clang of a bell telling them when to eat, pray, work or sleep. For heinous crimes such as whistling, they were sent to punishment cells with no light, no sound, no human contact and little food, all the better to reflect on their misdemeanours.

It was in this hell on earth, roasted in summer and frozen in winter, that the condemned spent their last days: men like Frederick Bailey Deeming, jewel thief, con man and bigamist, who killed his first wife and four children in Liverpool, killed his second in Melbourne and, masquerading as the dashing Baron Swanson, was just about to marry his third when he was arrested in 1892. His death mask, handsome even yet, still sits in his cell, as do the masks of all the final inhabitants of these tiny, doomed spaces; mute icons of the Victorian obsession with phrenology as a key to unlocking the dark secrets of criminal genetics.

Deeming, of course, is not the most famous man to be hanged here. That honour goes to Ned Kelly – who today in Australia is viewed as either a folk hero or a sadistic thug, depending on who you ask – the bushranger whose iron armour failed to save him when, in 1880, he was wounded and finally captured by what he memorably described as the 'ugly, fat-necked, wombat-headed, big-bellied, magpie-legged, narrow-hipped, splay-footed sons of Irish bailiffs or English landlords … known as Victoria Police'. After carefully nursing him back to health so that he was well enough to die, the prison authorities sent him to the gallows, where his last words were, 'Such is life'.

However, the real tragedy of Melbourne was not the Pentonville System, nor even the death of Ned Kelly. For weeks I had been looking forward to seeing the lamb chop in the National Gallery representing the proud centuries of sheep farming which, along with wheat, had formed the twin pillars of early Australian economy. As you can imagine, it was in a state of some excitement that I pulled up outside and strode manfully up to the entrance. Only to discover that it had closed five minutes earlier.

It was the greatest disaster of unfulfilled expectation since I had set out one day years before to find the world's only Kazoo Museum in New York State, and arrived five minutes too late for that as well. Now, as then, I pressed my nose hopelessly against the glass doors, feeling like a child locked forever out of the toyshop of dreams.

Still, at least we had an even bigger toy to look forward to the next day as we were going to Hallam, home of the Irving Vincent, a modern equivalent of the 1946 Vincent Series B Rapide. The latter had been designed by the Australian genius Phil Irving, and was the fastest production bike of its day, so in 1999 brothers Ken and Barry Horner sat down in a back room of their engineering works north of Melbourne to design a machine which would be a tribute to both Irving and the machine he designed. They succeeded to the extent that it won the Daytona Twins Championship against the big guns from Ducati and Yamaha, and the bikes are now for sale to any collector with one hundred grand to spare.

'All we need's a few rich stupid blokes,' said Ken, meeting us outside and leading us past Chip the office cockatoo, through the works and up to a machine which was possibly the most beautiful motorcycle I had ever seen – a perfect marriage of science and art, old and new.

After half an hour during which Ken said about three words, since to describe him as laconic would fall far short of the truth, we walked, drooling gently, out past Chip to get back into Matilda and return to Melbourne, with Gareth driving and Matt filming out the window.

Sadly, our peaceful journey was interrupted when there was a huge bang and all the warning lights on the dashboard came on. Closer examination revealed that the radiator had boiled over, so we let everything cool down, topped it up and phoned John at Wicked HQ in Brisbane.

'No worries, mate. Get her over to Jamie and his magic torch at our Melbourne depot, and he'll sort her out,' he said.

Dropping Colin off on the way through town so that he could buy a mobile phone, before long we were standing with

Jamie and his magic torch, gazing at Matilda's innards. Being Australian, he hadn't even bothered with the sharp intake of breath compulsory with mechanics everywhere else in the world.

'I'd be happier if she had a new radiator, boys. Temperature in Western Australia kills even new cars, and you don't want to break down out there. I'll organise a new one for you in Sydney,' he said. We shook hands and drove back to the hotel, keeping a careful eye on the temperature gauge, to find Colin inspecting his new mobile phone.

'Here, mate, how do you find your own phone number on this?' he said.

'It should be on a sticker on the box, or on a piece of paper inside,' I said.

'Nah, no sign of it.'

'Well, then text me, and it'll come up on my phone.'

'How do you send a text on these things?'

'Doesn't it say in the instructions?'

'Haven't read them, mate. I'm a bloke. By the way, can I borrow your socket adapter to charge this up?'

'I thought you had one.'

'Did. Think I left it in Apollo Bay, mate.'

Before I could beat him slowly to death with a telephone directory, he wandered next door to see Gareth, who found the number in five seconds. It was on the piece of paper in the box marked YOUR NUMBER in big letters, believe it or not.

Colin wisely chose that moment to go out and get an adapter and to find a print shop to get some flyers printed up with the trip website on them. And came back two hours later with some dental floss.

Still, I proved just as useless when I tried to recoup the expedition expenses by panning for gold in Ballarat, an hour's drive north through green and pleasant hills and the town that grew up around the 1850 discovery of gold in the area. It is a wonderful irony that the Victorian splendour of Melbourne, with its ornate mansions, afternoon teas and grand balls, was founded on gold-mining – one of the toughest, dirtiest and most dangerous occupations known to man.

As if to make matters worse, the authorities charged miners up to thirty shillings a month for a licence without providing anything in return, a situation which came to a head in 1854 when two hundred diggers led by Irishman Peter Lalor barricaded themselves behind an improvised stockade and refused to pay the licence fee. Thirty-five died in the resulting shoot-out, but Lalor went on to become a Member of Parliament and the Eureka Stockade Rebellion, as it became known, became an icon of two crucial elements of what it meant to be Australian.

One was the casting off of colonial shackles, as the domestic servants of Melbourne fled north to make their fortunes, leaving their masters and mistresses to make their own bloody tea.

And another was the tendency to stick with your mates against authority, to the extent that the Eureka Flag, a white cross and five stars on a blue background, remains to this day a symbol of left-wing protest.

It was fluttering against a cloudless sky as I walked up the slope to Sovereign Hill, the recreated 1850s mining settlement where I spent the afternoon chatting to assorted town drunks, redcoats, saloon keepers, genteel ladies, coachmen and miners, before trying my hand at panning in the nearby stream, which was where most miners had started before having to dig deeper and deeper in search of nuggets.

Half an hour later, I had uncovered a single fleck worth three dollars which would be barely enough to pay for the petrol to take me back to Melbourne.

While Geoff was off making his fortune, I decided to take Matt on a whistlestop tour of Brighton and St Kilda, the places where I had lived, grown up and hung out as a boy.

It was quite an emotional journey too, as the first stop was my old street, a place I hadn't seen since the late seventies when I had left home. Our old house had sat at the end of a cul-de-sac, but was now gone – demolished to make way for sports facilities for a local school, which gives some indication of the size of the place we had to run around in as kids.

A big ramshackle old place – a wooden home from the nineteenth century with a tin roof and a verandah that ran all around the front – it had once been the farmhouse for the area and we grew up with a huge garden full of fruit trees. The land around the house was so big that I even had a motorcycle track in the backyard where I could get up to third gear on my little dirt bike, much to my mum's eternal frustration. We were a wild bunch, and how she managed to put up with us is still beyond me, even though I am now a parent myself. Once we saw a knife-thrower on telly and within about five minutes, I had my sister Liese, who had volunteered to be my brave assistant, up against the wooden wall of what used to be stables with a chalk circle drawn around her. I then proceeded to throw my Bowie knives at her. It was probably more through luck than skill that she survived unscathed, though I do remember her long hair being pinned to the wall by one of the knives.

I also had an air rifle which we used to shoot cans and bottles, so cats and possums soon learned to avoid our place – especially as our Dobermann, Gretchen, who was the seventh member of our clan, had a particular fondness for disemboweling the poor creatures, a feat she once showed off in front of mum's guests at one of her rare dinner parties – the poor woman could do nothing civilised with us around.

With the beach at our doorstep, we could get up to all sorts of mischief down there as well – like diving off the pier into shallow water and skimming the bottom, a practice which I had down to an art form as I knew the seabed like the back of my hand.

We didn't have much money, but we were all very happy there. In fact, half of the rich kids in the neighbourhood gathered at our place for the fun. Every one of us still considers that house our childhood home and on the rare times that we are all able to get together, we relive the escapades we used to get up to.

After that it was off to my old mate Gus's place for a visit. Gus and I go way back to our teens, when we used to live around the corner from each other. We were pretty close, and together we got into all sorts of scrapes. We worked together and even shared a house at one stage, so we really were more like brothers than friends – except we probably got on better than most siblings. I also knew his wife Donna while we were growing up, as we all moved in the same circles.

Gus and Donna had declared open house and invited us all to a barbie at their place, in the now-trendy suburb of East St Kilda. It was perfect – the barbie was on, the beer was cold, and there was a football final on the telly that night to share with old mates. Heaven on a stick!

Yes, it's true – Colin had stunned us all by producing not one, but half a dozen real friends, including his old school pal Gus, a tearaway who had turned his destructive teenage talents into a lucrative career in demolition.

'Gus and I counted any night out when we came home rather than ending up in jail as a success,' said Colin, handing out the beers.

'Or a failure,' said Gus, who after working his way through every banned substance on the planet, had finally settled down and married Donna, a former model who at an age when most women were heading south still had the face and body of a twenty year old.

Sadly, just as Colin dispelled the myth of his imaginary friends, we found ourselves losing a real one. Gareth had reached the end of his three weeks with us, and so left halfway through the barbie for the overnight sleeper to Sydney and his flight home.

We would all miss him, not just for being chief stills

photographer, driver, caterer, IT helpdesk, assistant cameraman and maker of the finest coffee and ham and cheese sandwiches in the known universe, but for being able to mimic any accent going.

Just as we missed Gloria, not just for her boundless optimism, but for the fact that out of one suitcase, she had managed to produce, by my estimation, 4,836 different outfits, all colour coordinated. Even more astonishing, she'd somehow managed at times to be wearing a different outfit at lunch than the one she'd set off in that morning, which I never was able to figure out.

For the rest of us, who looked like refugees from the Albanian branch of Oxfam, it was deeply impressive.

The next day, the three of us that were left – me, Colin and Matt – rose early and rode north heading for the city of Canberra. Our journey took us along a tree-lined highway through rolling parkland which had climbed to high sierras by the time we stopped for a break at noon. As we sat in the shade outside a roadhouse, three Harley riders rolled in and walked inside with a nod.

'So sad the way middle-aged men feel the need to go riding around on motorbikes so they can feel like heroes,' I said.

'Aye, what's that all about?' said Matt.

'Beats me,' said Colin, and we rode on, passing some wonderful old cars out for a Sunday drive – an acid-yellow Ford V8, a purple Valiant, an endless black Cadillac with fins and whitewall tyres, and a silver E-Type convertible. Australia, like California, is a land where the climate is kind to ancient metal.

The afternoon stretched on, languid and hot, and to stop myself from nodding off, I kept myself amused by spotting road signs such as 'Gordon Exit Here', and wondering how many Gordons had exited, then wondered why; or 'Howlong This Exit', and muttering happily to the inside of my helmet, 'Not so long, thanks for asking'.

We were now heading into Kelly Country, the high country region in the north east of the state where Ned and his gang had their base. From there they had robbed banks in various towns and shot it out with the police on numerous occasions.

We passed the town of Glenrowan where, on 28 June 1880, the Kellys had made their last stand. Holed up with his gang inside a hotel, and clad in his famous armour, Ned had ordered some of his sympathisers to tear up a section of the railway track to prevent local police from getting reinforcements. When this plan failed, Ned rushed out and told his supporters to disperse, but it was too late. Police had surrounded the hotel, trapping Ned's brother Dan and mates Steve Hart and Joe Byrne inside. Ned then made a bold, but ultimately futile, attempt to rescue his friends, but they did not survive the siege.

Having left the others behind, I pulled off the highway to have a look around Glenrowan and, coming into the village, was greeted by a twenty-foot Ned in full armour, carrying a rifle.

I bought a Ned T-shirt and took a few pictures of the menacing figure, reflecting all the while on his last words 'Such is life' and thinking of my own future and what it might hold. Shaking off my melancholy thoughts, I fired Rosie up, and left Ned behind on guard, dipping my own helmet in salute. He and his gang had advocated that North East Victoria become a republic – if they had succeeded, this may well have been a separate state today.

Kelly may have been the most infamous of the lot, but other bushrangers also operated around here. For decades it was seen as beyond the reach of the law – a bit like south Armagh during the Troubles I suppose – but nowadays the area is peppered with ski resorts, and people come up in the summer to the alpine villages to escape the searing heat.

There are a lot of Irish place names in this region – I even noticed a place called Boho, the County Fermanagh village my mother had lived in as a child. Many left the Fermanagh village during the famine, and subsequent waves of immigration, so it seems likely that this is where some ended up.

We crossed the Murray River into New South Wales – our third state on the trip.

One of the largest and most complex constructions in Australia. And the Sydney Opera House.

7

It was when I found myself humming 'The Holly and the Ivy' that I realised it was time to stop for the day, which we did in a town called Albury – a pleasantly shady Victorian town so laid back that when it looked for another town to twin with, it looked no further than Wodonga which lies just half a mile away, across the Murray River.

We found a room at the ivy-clad Seaton Arms Motor Inn, whose very name conjured up images of excited honeymoon couples motoring north from Melbourne in their second-hand Model T looking forward to a fine steak dinner in front of a roaring fire followed by a night of freshly wedded bliss and waking together to the kookaburras chattering in the trees outside.

At a little Italian restaurant nearby, we certainly dined a lot better than explorer Gerard Krefft, who passed through these parts in 1857, captured alive several specimens of the rare pig-footed bandicoot, then got so hungry he ate them, shortly after which the species became extinct.

'They are very good eating, and I am sorry to confess that my appetite ... over-ruled my love for science,' he wrote shamefacedly in his journal.

As I sat tucking into spaghetti alla carbonara, it was obvious that we had left the urban coastline for farming country: lean and bronzed had become stocky and sunburnt; raw silk dresses and straw hats had become jeans, tattoos and baseball caps trumpeting the merits of assorted sheep dips; and vintage classics for the evening cruise had become supercharged hot rods straight out of *American Graffiti*.

For us Albury's main merit had been that it was exactly halfway between Melbourne and Canberra; at least so I had thought until I went for a constitutional the next morning and found the glass window of a hotel lobby lined with mint classic cars: a Jaguar E-Type, a Chevrolet Corvette Stingray, a Rolls-Royce, a Riley, an MG and a stately Jaguar Mark VII.

'Oh, the bloke who bought the building thought he may as well stick his car collection in the window while he got around to renovating the hotel,' said a passing housewife in answer to the question I hadn't asked her.

I wandered back to the Seaton Arms to find Matt packing up and Colin, obviously inspired by the example of Krefft, finishing off his breakfast then the last of his left-over pizza from the night before. Still, I suppose we should be grateful that he hadn't followed the example of another explorer, Edward Brinkmann who, after getting separated from his party and dog in a vicious storm in the nearby mountains in 1862, wandered around lost for three weeks before stumbling into Albury 'in a deplorable condition, having been without food and clothes for some time', according to his distraught companion, the German scientist Georg Balthasar von Neumayer.

Before long we were speeding north through wooded hills and surprisingly lush meadows in which grazed plump Aberdeen Angus cattle, blissfully unaware that their future could be summed up in three words: moo, bang, sizzle.

 Not long out of Albury, we made a stop at the Ettamogah pub, a recreation of the pub featured in the famous Ken Maynard cartoon series, first published in the *Australasian Post* magazine in 1958. It was a larrikin version of life in the outback, with singlet-wearing shearers, smoking dogs and all kinds of madcap adventures – always with a dry bush wit twist. Just about every Aussie family got the *Post* every week, including us, so the cartoons were well known. The pub was built by a man who came to Ettamogah looking for the famous watering hole, found there wasn't one and decided to build it himself, just as it appeared in the cartoons. So today, here it stands – not a straight wall in the place but still a major tourist attraction that serves great cold beer.

Continuing on up the Hume Highway we next came to Holbrook, also known as the submarine town. It had previously been called Germanton, but given the depth of feeling against the Germans during the First World War, it is not surprising that, in 1915, the townspeople elected to change the name. With patriotic feelings running high, the people chose Holbrook, after First World War hero Lt Commander Norman Holbrook, who sank a Turkish battleship in the Dardenelles – the same campaign that saw Australian and Irish troops being decimated at Gallipoli. There's a replica of Holbrook's B11 submarine in a park, also named after him, as well as a full-size representation of one of the Australian navy's modern subs, despite the town being hundreds of miles from the sea.

We had decided to stop at Holbrook because it was home to two bakeries that allegedly made the best pies in all of Australia. On the right side of the main street, according to our guidebook, was the old faithful Holbrook Bakery, serving that Aussie classic of beef and curry pie, while facing it was young pretender The Scrummy Buns Bakery, dishing up such avant garde delicacies as pies filled with crocodile, emu, kangaroo and rabbit.

Sadly, we arrived to find that The Scrummy Buns had gone the way of all things, so with the great pie showdown a non-starter, we contented ourselves with a Magnum bar and rode on to Canberra.

On the way we passed through the town of Gundagai, a town made famous by the many songs that have been written about it. One of these songs, 'Five Miles from Gundagai' references one of the town's statues, of a dog sitting on a tuckerbox – an iconic image that has its origins rooted in the time of the early pioneers. While the men would work they would often leave a dog to sit and guard their tuckerbox and possessions. The song is a celebration of that time and way of life. Another song, 'The Road to Gundagai', was sung by homesick Aussie troops during the Second World War, so music really is responsible for the notoriety of this town.

It's a neat little town too, with the main street running up on the side of a hill, lined with substantial hotels with balconies that stretch out over the wide footpaths to provide shade below and living space above. And there's a reason for the town being on a hill.

It used to be below on the alluvial flats at the conjunction of the Murrumbidgee, Murray and Lachlan rivers below and, despite the warnings of the local aboriginal people about building there in the first place, the settlers refused to move and so, in 1852 when the plain flooded, seventy-eight people were recorded drowned. It was Australia's worst natural disaster, until the raging bushfires in 2009.

Despite their advice being ignored, two aboriginal men risked their lives to rescue more than forty people from the raging torrent using their flimsy traditional canoes. They are justly celebrated as the heroes of the flood. After that, the town citizens belatedly decided to take the advice of the original locals and moved the town uphill. Gundagai also possesses some of Australia's longest and oldest wooden bridges, built to cross the now-respected flood plain.

We were now just an hour away from Canberra, the federal capital, a place I had been through but had never stopped in, as like most Aussies, I consider it a place full of politicians and their lackeys, and so best avoided.

In fact, my friends and I had once felt so disparagingly about it that we used to have 'Canberra wakes' for other mates who were public servants and were then transferred to the city. It's a feeling that is still prominent, as I had discovered at Gus and Donna's barbie.

'Why the hell are you going to Canberra?' people at the barbie had asked us, with the usual Aussie bluntness.

'It's a shithole, full of politicians and public servants and fuck all else.'

Of course as soon as I'd agreed, they all started defending it.

'Well, it has the National Gallery – that's worth a look, and the Federal Parliament is a pretty nice building, and up on the tower in the hills you get a great view, so it's not that bad I reckon.'

The real reason we were deviating off Highway One, and going to what is jokingly termed 'the dead centre of Australia', was actually to interview the national expert on the Irish/Australian diaspora, Dr Richard Reid, who was currently staging the biggest-ever display on the subject at the National Museum.

Dr Reid, it turned out, was another Ten Pound Tourist, coming originally from Portrush and, as he had arrived at around the same time as me in the very early 1970s, we compared notes.

The rest of our interview with Dr Reid was fascinating, but I won't reveal it here; not so you watch the TV series, but because it wasn't the best part of the museum for me. No, that was playing the wobble board along to a video of Rolf Harris singing 'Tie Me Kangaroo Down, Sport'.

Canberra was much as we had anticipated, given that it is a town built solely for the incredibly stupid reason that Sydney and Melbourne couldn't agree which should be the capital. In this, it is not alone, since Canada has Ottawa and Brasil has Brasilia, and it is as dull as you would expect a town filled with politicians to be. Still, at least it keeps them all in one place so the rest of us can avoid them. Construction started in 1913, but as you'd expect from a combination of politicians and builders, didn't really get going until 1958.

We had spent the morning exploring the only other real attraction in the city – the new parliament building, which looks like a Neolithic burial mound about to blast off into space. Not that the building was even the real highlight of our trip there. That honour goes to the magnificently Australian conversation we had with the policeman who arrived on his mountain bike as I was getting off the Triumph.

'G'Day, mate. Listen, if you park there, it means a fine for you and a shitload of paperwork for me. But if you park over there, it means none of the above, and we're both apples. Nice bike, by the way. Used to have a Bonnie, but these days I've got a nice little Yamaha ...'

By teatime, after a long hot ride through forested hills that at one stage opened to a vast grassy plain which looked like cow nirvana, but had not a beast in it from horizon to horizon, I was in Bowral, having taken a diversion out of curiosity not only to ride down a main thoroughfare called Bong Bong Street, but to take a look at the Bradman Museum, a tribute to the legendary cricketer Don Bradman who was born here and who went on to break every record in the game and defeat with immense courage the notorious English bodyline bowling of the thirties.

'Here, how come they've got his bat here, but not his balls?' I said to an old-timer as I wandered around the displays of the great man's memorabilia.

'Not enough room in the museum, mate,' he grinned. It was a perfectly Australian answer.

 While Geoff took his detour to Bowral, Matt and I remained on the Hume for a fairly uneventful ride to the town of Mittagong in the Blue Mountains outside Sydney. It's high plains country and the locals are big on their horses, utes, and two types of music – country and western.

The scenery is rugged and, like everything here, on a grand scale.

The people here seemed a bit more conservative than those we had met so far, and we had our first disparaging comments about the slogan painted on the back of Matilda. We promised to amend it and slid quietly into our hotel room to make our plans to invade Sydney the next morning – St Patrick's Day. We could almost taste the free Guinness that people would buy us for coming all the way from Belfast to celebrate with them. At least, so we hoped.

I met up with the guys in our motel in Mittagong, finished my work for the day and went out to bring back burgers and fries, which Colin polished off and then made not one, but two, toasted sandwiches while he watched *Around the World in Eighty Days* to pick up some handy adventuring hints.

Matt was downloading pictures to the website, and since we were due in Sydney the next day, I was lying in bed reading Robert Hughes' *The Fatal Shore* about the reasons why the convicts ended up there.

The reasons were several: but the most significant was the population explosion in Britain in the eighteenth century which saw the number of people in London alone double between 1750 and 1770, and created mass unemployment, especially among the young.

Fearing a crime wave, the government passed a series of increasingly draconian laws, culminating in the Waltham Black Act which made even petty offences such as poaching a rabbit, cutting down a bush or appearing in public with a dirty face a hanging offence.

Not surprisingly, this led to an explosion in the number of convicts who, when the jails ran out of space, were kept in rotting ships on the Thames or sent to America until the civil war made that impossible, making Australia the next obvious option.

I closed the book and fell asleep, and by lunchtime the next day we were riding through the rolling grasslands west of Sydney, a city first discovered in 1813 by settlers Gregory Blaxland, William Lawson and W.C. Wentworth, who after three weeks' struggle gazed down on a vista which they described as a cross between Arcadia and the land of Canaan, with enough pasture to support the stock of the colony for thirty years.

It was slightly less Arcadian for the convicts who were sent out to build the Great Western Road that leads to the city, working in irons that finally wore through their flesh to the bones. As the convict memoirist Thomas Cook put it:

> With a sheet of bark for my bed, the half of a threadbare blanket for my covering, and a log for my pillow, the action of the frost was so severe on my limbs that it was with difficulty I could find the use of them, and then only by frequenting the fire at intervals during the night.
>
> As I arose, after experiencing all the horrors of a restless and perishing cold night, the rugged mountains covered with the snow, and the frozen tools for labour stared me in the face before the stars were off the skies; and many a tear did I shed, when contemplating upon my hard fate, and the slight offence for which I had been doomed to participate so largely in the bitters of a wretched life.

Such horrors seemed unimaginable as we rode down what was now a six-lane highway and saw for the first time the glories of Sydney: the great coathanger of the Harbour Bridge, the Opera House, like a whispering of nuns, and beyond them the reason the city came into being in the first place, the perfect harbour of Port Jackson.

In January 1788 the First Fleet, commanded by Arthur Phillip and carrying over a thousand people, 736 of them convicts, moored in Botany Bay south of here, expecting the fine meadows that Captain James Cook had described eight years before.

However, either they had landed in a slightly different place, or Cook had been unduly optimistic in his description, as they found nothing but swamp, scrub and sand. Undeterred, they sailed a couple of miles north and found this sheltered bay, cosseted by wooded hills and a freshwater stream, and celebrated by breaking out both the rum and convicts for the night, leading to the mother of all orgies.

The next morning, of course, they woke to the mother of all hangovers, and over the next three years nearly starved to death as they tried and failed to establish farms to feed the budding colony.

Mind you, it was hardly surprising: since the only thing the convicts had in common was that they were small-time criminals, you could hardly have picked a worse bunch to found a colony. Although they would need to grow their own crops and catch their own fish, they had one gardener, and he was only twenty years old, and a single fisherman. And although they would need houses, there were only six carpenters, two brickmakers, two bricklayers, a mason and no sawyers.

Against all these odds, by the early nineteenth century, Sydney, named after the Viscount who was Secretary of State back home, had grown into a busy port, with the Army officers who brought the convicts out becoming rich farm owners on a combination of free land and cheap labour, eventually becoming powerful enough to mutiny against the Governor, a certain Captain Bligh, in 1809. Yes, that Captain Bligh.

Bligh was sent packing and replaced by the liberal reformer Lachlan Macquarie, whose vision of an elegant, prosperous city was not dampened by the refusal of London to provide funds. Instead, Macquarie simply hired architect Francis Greenway, a former convict, and paid him with rum money which came from a monopoly on liquor sales.

The result was the splendour of Hyde Park, College Street and Macquarie Street through which we rode, gazing up in awe until we came at last to Bondi Beach, where we gazed around in even more awe at one of the most hedonistic scenes on the planet.

It was almost impossible to imagine that this same spot was once populated by people who, after months of horror getting here, then faced years of even greater horror when they arrived in a penal colony where a man could be given one hundred lashes for smiling. It was a place so horrific that men would blind themselves to be taken off the endless back-breaking toil, and when convicts were sentenced to hang for some petty offence or other, they often wept with joy, whereas those who were spared to return to a chain gang wept with despair.

One mentally disturbed eighteen year old, Charles Anderson, was lashed for repeated escape attempts then finally chained to a rock for two years, his unhealed back in constant agony from maggots. Remarkably, after being freed by Alexander Maconochie, a new and more humane governor, Anderson became a model citizen.

When we arrived in Bondi we were greeted by Angeline O'Neill, a native of Randalstown, County Antrim, who has set up a luxury Bed and Breakfast in the beachside suburb. Dressed all in green as a nod to St Patrick's Day, she made us very welcome, while down on the beach, and at Bondi junction, hundreds of Irish travellers, and those natives who claim some or no Irish ancestry, were packing out the pubs, as diddly-dee music echoed around the streets.

Many Aussies take the day, or at least part of it, off to celebrate, though they actually get two days to party as the official parade is always held on the nearest Sunday to the actual day and the celebrations get bigger with each year that passes.

I took a ride along the famous Bondi beach where tanned, bikini-clad young women paraded around with their buff boyfriends; skaters and skateboarders skated; and the surfers caught some reasonably tame waves. We even managed to come across a real-life rescue which was being filmed for the reality TV show, *Bondi Rescue* – a series shown all around the world.

A young guy had been struggling in deep water, after being pulled out by the rip, but the lifesavers raced to the scene on their beach quads, and one took to the water on a long surfboard to pull him out. His friends had stood on the beach, hands to their mouths in horror as the scene unfolded. Right behind them stood the film crew, camera focused on the action while a sound man dangled a boom mike over them to catch their panicked conversation.

The funny thing about Bondi is that at least half the people here are tourists and backpackers just passing through for a week, a month or a year. Many Sydneysiders speak of it disparagingly, preferring the ocean beaches further out of the city, but to our eyes it looked like paradise.

Dancing with wolves is so last week.
Walking with wombats is where it's at.

8

'Here, Tim, it's not really true what Colin told me about seven out of the ten most dangerous creatures in the world being in Australia, is it?' I said as we walked through the front door of the Australian Reptile Park the next day and shook hands with head mammal keeper Tim Faulkner.

'Nah, of course not, mate,' said Tim with a grin while crushing several of the smaller bones in my hand in a friendly kind of way. 'It's more like ten out of ten, and I'm just about to introduce you to all of them.'

Naturally, I took this bad news like a man and started sobbing, at which Tim decided that I needed to be broken in gently to the dangers of the outback. As a result, five minutes later I found myself cuddling a baby wombat called Wanda, before taking her for a walk, which proved more difficult than I imagined, since she stuck so closely to my ankles that every time I stopped I was in severe danger of squashing her flat and spending the rest of my days in the Ned Kelly Memorial Cell in Melbourne Gaol for unjustifiable wombaticide.

Having conquered that hurdle, it was only a matter of time before I was face to face with a funnel-web spider, whose bite can kill you in an hour, and a Fierce Snake, whose venom is so toxic that one tiny nibble from its fangs will kill a million of the mice he lives on in the desert.

Why it needs such a staggering degree of toxicity is not known, but it is far from alone in Australia; the Box Jellyfish, whose merest touch creates pain which the few who have survived it liken to holding a white-hot poker against your skin for several hours, or until you faint if you're lucky, has enough poison in its system to kill a large house party.

As does the Blue-Ringed Octopus, the Stonefish and a dozen other species lurking out there. In fact, in Australia, even seashells can kill you: annoy a cone shell and you'll have a handful of venomous pincers before you can say, 'Gosh, an angry seashell. That's a bit of a surprise, and no mistake.'

All of which made me wonder why at this moment I had a ten-foot python curled around my neck whispering sweet nothings in my left ear, and ten minutes later found myself with a Tasmanian Devil under each elbow growling sweet nothings into my armpits.

Tim's pride and joy are those two hand-reared Tasmanian Devil cubs, as the park is part of a nation-wide programme to try and save the animal from extinction. The species is being devastated by a contagious cancer which creates tumours on the animal's face and leaves it unable to eat, resulting in it starving to death.

'Their gene pool is so small that they are essentially all related, so when they get together the disease spreads as they have no immunity to it.'

Tim and his colleagues are also trying to dispel some of the myths surrounding the creatures, and, as we cuddled them and stroked their soft fur, it was hard to reconcile the gentle creatures we held with all the fearsome tales. According to Tim, the Devils were only given their name because of the guttural growls and screams they made at night which terrified the first settlers.

'They are actually quite timid creatures as you can see,' said

Tim. 'If these were real wild Devils, they'd be so frightened they wouldn't even move, but would remain rooted to the spot. They live solitary, yet communal lives, as they all go off and do their own thing, but use common latrine areas to keep in touch. They are scavengers, and all those tales about them bringing down cattle and sheep are just that, tales – Warner Brothers and the Taz cartoons have a lot to answer for.'

Their undeserved reputation notwithstanding, Tim did warn us that the Devils had extremely powerful jaws and so had a pretty fearsome bite, 'Pound for pound, they have probably the strongest jaws in the world and even the bite from one this size would be equivalent to that from an American pit bull.'

Even Australia's cuddly creatures had a serious side it seemed.

Their work with the Devils is not the only important job that Tim and his colleagues do at the park, as he demonstrated when we witnessed him milking a Tiger Snake. As Tim explained, while the park was open to the public and valued its guests, serious work was done there supplying venom from all types of deadly creatures so that it could go off to be used in making antidotes.

'We're in the business of saving lives – just last week in Sydney alone, three people were bitten by snakes in a period of less than three hours, so what we do here is vital.'

Tim clearly loves his animals though and defended the snakes, explaining that most people get bitten through their own stupidity and ignorance.

'It's usually a case of idiots showing off when they've had too many beers. They'll see a snake and try to pick it up, or something like that. A snake will only bite if it is cornered – it just wants to get away.'

Tim then proudly showed us Elvis, the five-metre salt-water crocodile who sat at the bottom of his pool, watched over by a keeper armed only with a long shovel handle, while another keeper trimmed the bushes in his enclosure. He was massive and Tim revealed that he had to be kept isolated as he'd eaten his last two girlfriends.

We joked that Elvis could get together with the rock wallabies and go on tour, though I suppose the last thing you want to hear on the PA system at this park are the words, 'Elvis has left the building'.

Leaving the park firmly established as a cross between Tarzan and St Francis of Assisi, I returned to Sydney and was writing on the balcony of Angeline's Bed and Breakfast when Colin flung a rubber snake into my lap from the garden below and undid all Tim's good work, the swine.

Angeline, an Irish backpacker hippie chick turned successful businesswoman, had offered us a couple of free nights in return for some publicity. Naturally, we told her it was completely impossible for us to sacrifice the innocent virgin of our journalistic principles on the satanic altar of commercial necessity, then realised how much it would save us, and said stuff the virgin.

For the next two days, we rested our weary heads on Egyptian cotton sheets, washed our dusty limbs under showers which were like the quality of mercy that droppeth from heaven upon the place beneath, snuggled into fluffy cotton towels and salved our dry throats in the morning with free-range organic Colombian coffee which had been picked then hand-knitted by blind widows on the slopes above Bogotá who had then been killed to ensure they took their secrets with them to the grave.

Out the back you could see the ocean, and out the front was a park which was busy from dawn to dusk with children and adults alike playing sport, confirming my belief that Australia is the healthiest nation on earth.

Sadly, after two days swanning around at Angeline's, some paying customers arrived and we had to return to the real world in the shape of the Sydney Harbour Youth Hostel, but even that proved to be a far cry from the youth hostels of my adolescence, with shiny staff, matching rooms and even en suite bathrooms, for heaven's sake.

'Can't understand why they don't have the rooms closer to the front door. And why you have to go up steps then down again to get to them,' said Colin as we carried the bags in.

'Oh do stop moaning, you bloody whingeing Aussie drongo,' I said cheerfully.

After dumping our gear in our rooms, we headed off to meet James Freeman, the organiser of the inaugural and brilliantly titled Shitbox Rally. The idea is that competitors have to buy a 'shitbox' car, spending less than $1,000 on the purchase, before driving it from Sydney to Alice Springs. They must also raise more than $3,000 to enter and when, or if, they get to Alice, the vehicles are auctioned off to raise more cash, if anyone is generous – or foolish - enough to buy them.

James came up with the idea in 2009 to raise money for a cancer charity after he lost both his parents to the disease within a few months of each other. When we met him, his phone was running red-hot as media interest in the quirky event had been sparked and he was doing interview after interview.

'I just started calling it the shitbox, as that's what the cars were – shitboxes. Then I sat down and tried to come up with a name that would describe what it was all about, and realised that the Shitbox Rally said it all, so that was it. It's not a race as such. We'll all be travelling in convoy really and if anyone breaks down or gets bogged, we'll all help each other out. We've got a few challenges on the way, but really it's going to be more about fun and meeting people and having a good time.'

He told us that around twenty teams had entered, a response which had amazed him.

'We've already had more than two hundred people wanting to join in next year's race, but we wanted to keep it manageable for this year to see how it goes but, all being well, next year the Shitbox will be full-on.'

Early next morning all three of us went down to Centennial Park to meet the lunatics who were ready to drive across the desert in their clapped-out old bangers. It was worth the Herculean effort. We met as bizarre and amusing a bunch of eccentrics as you could hope to find outside of the funny farm.

There was a bunch of lads with their mum's twenty-five-year-old runabout, painted up to look like one of the interceptor cars in the *Mad Max* movies, with the guys also in costume and character.

'It's not about the car,' they told us. 'It's all about looking cool and getting the chicks.'

As if on cue, two Penelope Pitstops from the old TV cartoon show, *The Wacky Races* – complete with pink dresses, white helmets, goggles and boots – turned up, and the boys made a beeline to intercept them.

Another two girls had customised their banger to look like a ladybird, while a couple in 'Shitty-Shitty-Bang-Bang' had gone for the eighties disco bling look, complete with gold and black tracksuits, medallions and headbands. After a barbie breakfast (what else?), the entrants posed for a group photo then climbed into their modified wrecks and headed for Alice Springs.

Our afternoon was taken up with a tour of Circular Quay, Sydney's main ferry terminal, which has the Harbour Bridge on one side and the Opera House on the other, with a constant flotilla of ferries and jet boats and other tourists attractions constantly plying back and forward – sort of like a maritime Heathrow.

We decided to get out on the water and take a trip around the harbour to get a sea-level view of the city. It was a great way to understand just how the city works and how vital the harbour is to both commerce and pleasure. My father used to live in the trendy north-shore suburb of Cremorne in Sydney and I had visited him there a few times. I was therefore reasonably familiar with the city. One of the things I loved most was travelling around by ferry – it has none of the stifling claustrophobia of buses and trains and using it to get to many of the city's attractions, like Taronga Zoo, is part of the experience.

We had a pleasant afternoon seeing all the sights from the water. A crowd of schoolboys from a college in Melbourne on a school excursion around the country joined us for part of the trip and their day was made when an attractive young woman sitting on the prow of a passing speedboat lifted her top and flashed them, causing much hilarity.

 Later that day we made our way to Deus Ex Machina, the motorcycle company operating from a renovated factory in Camperdown, Sydney.

All devotees of Greek and Latin drama, which I'm sure includes all of you, will know that the phrase *Deus Ex Machina* means 'God from the machine', and is a device used by crap playwrights when they realise they've only got one minute to go in the last act and no denouement in sight. Solution: enter God stage-left with magic wand, and all sorted.

He'd certainly been busy inside Deus, I thought as we wandered around looking at bog-standard bikes which had been transformed into works of art. Two of the men behind this magic are Dare Jennings, who used to run the surf-clothing giant Mambo before he and a couple of friends started Deus in 1996, and head of sales Shaun Zammit.

'Here, are your parents from the planet Krypton, or do you guys just pick your names out of a Superman comic?' I said to Shaun as we stood looking at a Triumph Thruxton, already my favourite bike in the world, which the mechanics at Deus had made even faster and more beautiful, a thing I had previously thought impossible.

'I could tell you, but then I'd have to kill you,' said Shaun, whose parents turned out, in fact, to be from Malta and Yorkshire.

'Fair enough. And how much will you sell me this for?'

'To you, $40,000, although we might take your Tiger in part exchange.'

I sighed deeply, and bought a T-shirt from the sale rack instead.

'Listen, dickhead,' I said cheerily to Colin as we got back on the bikes, 'can you stop racing off at a hundred miles an hour in the wrong direction for a change, and follow Matilda, since she has the directions back to the youth hostel in the sat nav?'

Naturally, he responded by racing off at a hundred miles an hour in the wrong direction. Then raced back in the right direction and overtook Matilda. When I finally caught him at the next red lights, I flipped up my helmet and shouted over, 'Here, you do know that following involves going behind, don't you?'

'Nah, you can follow from the front, mate,' he said – a koan riddle which would have baffled even the most ardent Zen Buddhist.

On the way back to the youth hostel, we passed the Captain James Cook Hotel, where the famous explorer stayed when he arrived here in 1770, and which was founded by his brother Thomas, who then went on to start his own travel company. Not many people know that, possibly because I just made it up.

Slightly less historic was the sign on the back of a bus advertising Gaytime ice lollies with the slogan 'You can't have a Gaytime alone'. This was quaint when the lollies first came out forty years ago, and has been even quainter since Sydney itself came out in the past two decades as one of the gayest cities in the world, culminating in a four-week Mardi Gras in February in which you will see, for example, a bunch of blokes dressed as nuns calling themselves the Sisters of Perpetual Indulgence wandering down the street while a lesbian motorcycle gang called Dykes on Bikes watches over them to make sure they're not attacked by Continuity Presbyterians Against This Sort of Thing.

That evening, I walked out of the front door of the youth

hostel, found a mixed volleyball tournament in progress in the sports centre across the road, and wandered in to spend half an hour vicariously reliving my youth. After about ten minutes, one of the matches finished and one of the Asian girls who had been playing wandered past, then sat down beside me.

'You play?' she said.

'Used to, about a million years ago.'

'Oh, I'm sure it wasn't that long ago,' she laughed. 'Where did you play?'

'Ireland, Holland, then semi-pro in Los Angeles after I left university.'

'Wow. You must have been good. You still look in shape.'

'You're very kind. Or short-sighted. I used to have the body of a Greek god, but these days it's more like a Greek temple. The Acropolis after the Turks blew it up, for example.'

'Well, if you're here next Friday, you're signed, although we can only pay you in beer.'

Sadly, by next Friday I was going to be somewhere north of Brisbane, so I shook hands with her and wandered down the street to the pub where we were due to meet up with Jennifer, a long-lost friend of Matt's and a rare example of that little-known species: the Glasgow blonde.

We were sitting outside the pub down the road under a tree sipping pints of that even less well-known Australian beer, Fat Yak, when there was a fluttering of giant wings overhead followed by a crashing sound and the see-sawing of leaves all around us.

'Fruit bat,' said Colin who had been up in my microlight once. 'Even worse landings than yours, and that's saying something.'

'Ah, as all aviators say, a perfect landing is one where you can walk away and the plane is reusable,' I said, as our supper arrived right on time.

'Song for the day, Geoff?' said Matt as we walked back to the youth hostel later.

'"Sisters of Mercy" by Leonard Cohen.'

'Disturbing. But acceptable.'

Geoff astride a 1937 Rudge Ulster

9

Sunday morning, and the bells of St Mary's Cathedral rang out to call the faithful few to prayer. In Hyde Park next door, the only ones there to hear them at first were the occasional jogger padding past the tidy lawns, flowerbeds and fountains, a few strolling ibis and a baffled man with a matching red setter. Before long though the streets all around were filled with forty shades of green, worn by people from all over the world who had become honorary Irishmen and women for the day to pay tribute to a Welsh shepherd called Patrick.

The parade was supposed to start at noon, but since we were running on Irish time for the day, it was well past the hour by the time the throng gathered outside the old town hall stopped random thronging and started thronging in one direction, passing as they did the former New South Wales Masonic Hall (now a boutique hotel), a massage parlour, a policeman taking his life in his hands by wearing an orange high-visibility vest, and a man selling T-shirts saying 'Leprechauns made me do it'.

Leading what is the biggest St Patrick's Day parade in the world after New York were a bunch of Irish dancers having a big-hair day, a brace of wolfhounds having a bad-hair day, a band mysteriously playing 'A Scottish Soldier', and the impromptu choir of The Jolly Irish Outdoor and Hiking Club of New South Wales, who were as enthusiastic as they were tone-deaf.

Behind them came the representatives of the various counties, of which Offaly was awfully small, Leitrim had picked up a job lot of sparkly emerald waistcoats and bowler hats from an Everything for a Dollar shop, Sligo had hijacked an Aston Martin Vantage, and Kilkenny were led by two Aboriginals playing didgeridoos who were later led away suffering from cultural confusion.

Cork, meanwhile, won the pizzazz prize of the day for a trailer with a giant slogan saying 'Ireland: 31 counties – then God created the People's Republic of Cork', and Wexford picked up the innovation award for an entire artificial ski slope, complete with blizzard, on the back of a float bearing the legend Wexford Bobsleigh Team, Vancouver 2010.

It was all the hokiest of fun, but strangely, as we walked away to get on the bikes and ride out of town, I felt an almost tangible sense of love and loss for home.

It was, in fact, appropriate that we left Sydney after the most Irish of days, since we were heading in the same direction as several gangs of Irish convicts who, on 1 November 1791, escaped and fled north into the bush, sure that if they walked far enough, they would reach China.

In spite of extensive research, I had failed to find a single reason for this belief other than a singularly Irish blend of optimism and surrealism. In any case, if they'd waited long enough, China would have come to them, for the streets of the city are full of delicate Oriental women strolling with small dogs and medium-sized men.

We stopped for a break in the searing heat of afternoon and, as I was sitting against a wall enjoying a Werther's Original and reading my research notes, I realised to my horror that in the excitement of St Paddy's Day I had completely failed in my plans to visit the plastic bag collection in the Hyde Park

Museum. Sob. First the kazoo museum, then the lamb chop, and now this. I would never make a proper adventurer, I thought, finishing my Werther's, climbing back on the bike and heading wearily north through heavily wooded hills.

I was still getting used to just how green this part of Australia was, since I had assumed that the entire country would consist of the Sydney Opera House and then the outback starting just after the city limits. Which just goes to show you what use assumption is.

In the blessed cool of late afternoon, we rolled up to the National Motorcycle Museum, a collection of sheds in the hamlet of Nabiac containing around eight hundred bikes, only to find a squadron of Harleys already there, surrounded by a gang of men, some of them with more tattoos and piercings than they had teeth, wearing tattered leathers and denims emblazoned with gang patches and badges.

As we got off the bikes, half of them stomped over, led by the biggest and fiercest looking. This is it, I thought. I've survived the hill bandits of Baluchistan, the drug barons of Colombia and a Saturday night in Sauchiehall Street in Glasgow, only for it all to end here.

'G'day,' said the leader of the gang. 'You the Irish blokes?'

'Er, yes,' I said nervously, all too aware that back in 1804, Newcastle just to the south of here had been founded for convicts too hard even for Sydney.

'Good on ya. Cheffie's the name,' he said, offering a meaty paw. 'We turned up late for the museum and they told us we could stay in the house around the back, except some Irish buggers had already booked it, so we thought it must be you. Here's me card.'

I took it. 'Ipswich Easy Riders: Adventure before Dementia', it said.

'Listen, Cheffie, if it's a house, I'm sure there's plenty of room for all of us,' I said.

'Nah, we'll just go down the pub and camp around the back,' he said.

The house in question turned out to be a rustic clapboard bungalow with a verandah and a meadow out the front. We finished our work for the day, then cooked up some pasta and had a beer on the verandah as the sun went down, feeling like Huckleberry Finn and Tom Sawyer.

And then we went to bed like boys on Christmas Eve and dreamt of Nortons. And Triumphs, of course.

Next morning, we were standing outside the door of the museum as owner Margaret Kelleher opened up. She and her husband Brian had run a bike shop in Canberra until Brian's motorcycle collecting habit became so bad that they realised they may as well start a museum with the four hundred and eighty machines he had stored in sheds he'd built with that staple of Aussie rural architecture, galvanised iron, or galvo as it is universally known.

Back then, bikers had such a bad reputation that every time Margaret and Brian went touring, they had to book ahead so that motel owners wouldn't run away screaming when they rolled up on two wheels.

'Then one day in the late nineties we arrived in Nabiac and everyone treated us like human beings, so we bought a plot of land and built the museum,' said Margaret. 'Here, what are you doing wearing a Deus Ex Machina T-shirt? Don't you know that most of their clients are gay men with more money than sense?'

'Well, I'm not gay, and I haven't got either,' I said. 'Anyway, it was reduced from $70 to $15.'

'$70 for a T-shirt? Bloody hell.'

Having sorted out Deus, she then led us on a happy hour around the eight hundred motorcycles in the collection, accompanied by her arthritic chihuahua, Acme.

The collection is vast with many examples of variations on the same models. They had at least four of the types of bikes I have owned and ridden over the years, and they even had a small selection of home-made bikes, just like the one that started me off when I was eleven years old. I was even more impressed when I saw the rare models that they had collected – like the 1920s Indian, or the Vincent Black Knight. They even had on display the remains of a Harley that was destroyed in the devastating bushfires of 2009 that had killed almost two hundred people.

The pride of their collection, however, was the Australian-built 47cc Yamaha-powered bike that broke land speed records for 50cc, 75cc and 100cc engines – Margaret, you see, is fiercely patriotic. In fact, she only buys Australian products unless she truly can't avoid it.

'Every bike here was made in the country,' she told us, 'and we never sell a bike. People make us offers but we just say no.'

For me, the most emotional moment was filming a piece for the documentary while sitting on a 1937 Rudge Ulster similar to the one my dad raced in the fifties, complete with ancient leathers, gauntlets and pudding bowl helmet. As I talked, I was filled with melancholy thinking of him as he is now at the age of eighty-four, 'old and grey and full of sleep', and of the man he was when he tore around circuits on motorcycles such as this, filled with vim and vigour in the days when he met and fell in love with my mother.

How sad it is, that we all grow old, I thought, then dealt with that sadness in the only way I know, by getting on a motorcycle and riding into the newborn day, holding aloft the torch of hope and optimism against the darkness of the unknown future and my own advancing years.

We rode north and, over the next few days, the landscape began to slowly change, with the Norfolk pines giving way to palms, the dry heat giving way to sultry damp, chrysanthemums in tidy gardens becoming the smack of bougainvillaea against an azure sky, and in the evenings, the thunder of trucks on the highway giving way to the wavering threnody of mosquitoes on the prowl.

As for the occasional towns and villages, they were straight out of an America of the fifties – the clapboard motor inns on the road in advertising 'TV!' 'Queen-Size Beds!' 'Pool!', the general stores and shady verandahs on the way through, and the gas stations on the road out.

Except for Frederickston, which had the added bonus of a giant sign advertising 'Fredo's Famous Pies! Fifty Varieties!' Incredibly, Colin rode right past it, so that I had to honk and point. He looked, wobbled, then rode back.

'Can't believe I missed that, mate,' he said, leading the way inside for a good three minutes of dithering before he picked the Truckie.

'Is that made of genuine truck drivers?' I said to the girl behind the counter.

'Sure is. And a bit of steak, bacon, onion and egg thrown in for no extra charge,' she said, handing it over.

Unable to decide between the camel and the crocodile, I had both. The crocodile, naturally, tasted of chicken, but the camel was like a curious blend of beef and lamb, so if you like the sound of that, here is Fredo's recipe for stuffed camel.

Ingredients
1 whole camel, medium
2 whole lambs, large
20 whole chickens, medium
2kg almonds
1kg pistachios
60 eggs
12kg rice
110 litres water
5kg black pepper

Method
Skin, trim and clean camel. Boil until tender.
Cook rice until fluffy.
Fry nuts and mix with rice.

Hard boil and peel eggs.
Stuff chickens with some of the eggs and rice.
Stuff lamb with some of the chickens and rice.
Stuff camel with lamb and remaining eggs.
Broil camel in large oven until brown.
(Note: not suitable for microwaving)

To serve
Spread remaining rice on large tray and place camel on top.
Place remaining stuffed chickens around camel.
Garnish with boiled eggs and nuts.

Serves 80–100

If that's too complicated, try Fredo's Elephant Stew.

Ingredients
1 elephant, medium
2 rabbits (optional)
salt
pepper
gravy

Method
Cut elephant into bite-sized pieces
Add enough gravy to cover.
Cook over bonfire for four days.

Serves 3,800

The menu now sorted for our next barbie, we rode on, and by teatime we were rolling into Coffs Harbour, a resort full of splendidly hokey attractions such as the giant banana, the originator of a series of giant lobsters, galahs, sheep, bulls, penguins, olives, mowers, mosquitoes, macadamia nuts, oysters, paperclips, rum bottles, gumboots and woolsacks. These gargantuan items have been placed in strategic places around the country, designed with one purpose in mind: to force small children in the back of the family Holden to scream as one, 'Dad, look, it's a GIANT KOALA! Let's stop right here so you can spend some of your hard-earned dollars on steak, eggs, vegetables boiled to buggery and koala fridge magnets, even if we don't have a fridge.'

Naturally, being more mature than all that, we just posed for photos with arms aloft, so that it looked as if we were holding up the giant banana.

Aussies became fascinated with 'big' objects back in the seventies and, as Geoff has said, there are dozens of them scattered around the country, usually themed on what the local district is known for – bananas, pineapples, sheep, cattle, fish or seafood. With a landscape dotted by banana and pineapple plantations and vast fields of sugar cane, it is not surprising that the giant banana was the monument of choice here, and it's not for nothing that Queenslanders are known as 'Banana Benders'.

Thickly-wooded mountains rise up between the valleys here and the road alternates between flat flood plains and curves and dips through forests of gum. We could feel it getting warmer and more humid as we got further north, until it felt definitely tropical. This part of the country – that is, the central coast of New South Wales – is known as the Great Lakes, as there are several in the area. A number of huge rivers, like the Manning, also flow into the lakes towards the sea and the whole region is a boating and fishing paradise.

As a result, Coffs Harbour has become a thriving tourist destination with people coming from all over the country for the fishing and watersports, as well as whale-watching in the winter. Its main attractions, in common with most places along this coast, are the beach, surfing, fishing and anything else to do with the water – all year-round activities thanks to the benign and predictable climate. One of its chief draws for families is the pet porpoise pool, where visitors can go swimming with the little cousins to the dolphin.

As if a giant banana wasn't enough excitement for one day, Coffs also had a motel in the shape of a windmill. Sadly, we had already booked into a normal one, where as I sat on the balcony typing the recipe for elephant stew, a two-foot lizard sat by my left elbow looking on with interest. It was so heartwarming to see reptiles taking in interest in cookery, even if all they eat is insects, just as it gladdens the soul to see penguins always dressing formally for dinner, even if all they eat is fish.

Talking of which, Colin arrived through the door five minutes later with supper from Hungry Jack's around the corner.

'Aussieburgers, mate. Steak, bacon, eggs, onions, beetroot, pineapple, tomatoes, red sauce and a slice of lettuce for veggies,' he said, and he wasn't joking.

Australia's fondness for beetroot, which you will find lurking in the most unexpected quarters, is just one of the throwbacks to the fifties which linger on, along with things like rotary clotheslines. Best of all, the clotheslines are called Hills Hoists. There is no apostrophe, it having been abandoned, along with the letter r, as an unnecessary post-colonial impediment.

Not surprisingly after our Aussieburgers, we slept like babies, except without the throwing up and the bedwetting, and were woken at dawn by a cacophony of sound and colour in the form of a dozen lorikeets lined up on the balcony singing their little hearts out.

'Wow, how beautiful,' I said.

'Noisy bastards,' said Colin, rolling over, farting and going back to sleep. Fortunately, when he regained consciousness, he remembered that we had to pay the toll for riding out of Sydney two days before. I'd made a mental note to remember it, then accidentally lost the note down the back of the virtual sofa in my head.

Somehow, it fell to me to sort this out, and after failing to get a wireless signal so I could do it online, I phoned the helpline and spent half an hour listening to thrilling messages telling me how important my call was to the Road Traffic Authority before I finally got through to a pleasant girl called Naomi, who dealt with it in no time.

'Listen, you've been a complete star. Thanks a million,' I said to her.

'No worries. At least you weren't yelling at me,' she said.

Outside, we were packing the bikes when a passerby came over and said, 'Here, I recognise those accents.'

He turned out to be Mike Cush from east Belfast, who'd emigrated here with his wife in the early seventies.

'I joined the police reserve in 1972 to try and make a difference, then discovered that both sides were trying to shoot me, and thought stuff that,' he said.

Five minutes out of town, I spotted a road sign saying Old Coast Road, went to investigate and, half a mile down the road, found a formerly elegant house which, from the faded sign, had also been a motor inn or café as well. The jungle had almost completely taken it back, and the only sign of life was a faded copy of the September 1969 issue of *House and Garden* on the verandah, with the cover offering 'A Perfect Rose Garden' and 'New Sofas From Old'.

Soon I was back on the main road where, five minutes later, I came across a model flying club, with a grass strip which would have been a credit to Robe Bowling Club, lined with half a squadron of men of a certain age, their brows gently knitted in benign concentration as they looped and rolled bijou Tiger Moths and Spitfires. You could not have asked for a more perfect counterpoint of women's desire to create harmony and beauty around them, and men's to test themselves either against each other or their own limits.

All men want to be heroes, you see, especially to their wives, but in their misguided minds, they think the way to do it is by going off and flying aeroplanes or riding motorbikes across continents, whereas the still, silent truth is that they would probably do it better by staying at home and doing the dishes.

And talking of dishes, several weeks after this, I read a wonderful thing in a magazine in Broome: that in Italian, the word for table, *tavola*, is masculine until the table is set, when it becomes feminine.

Meanwhile, I rode on along the Pacific Highway, though it's a bit of misnomer to call it this as it runs quite a bit inland due to all the river crossings it has to make. We had a bit of time up our sleeves that day, so I just took it slow and enjoyed the scenery along the road – lush sub-tropical forests, massive rivers and quaint old towns that looked as if they could be sets for a production of *Huckleberry Finn*. Indeed, some of the rivers were so massive they could have doubled for the Mississippi, yet despite being educated in Australia, I had never heard of most of them, like the Richmond River, which makes the Thames look like a tributary.

The effects of the recent devastating rains further north in Queensland could be seen everywhere, as every river and creek was running high and tree branches were stroking the smooth, yet fast-flowing water. Many of the cane fields were like rice paddies and we saw one parked car with water up to its axles – another reason besides the heat to build homes on stilts.

By this stage Geoff had caught up with us, just in time for us to run into some roadworks. 'Think we're gonna get pretty wet soon' the ganger holding the stop/go pole told us.

We told him we already had. Twice. But that we had just laughed it off as the rain was warm, plus we were hard-assed bikers who feared nothing but a lack of pies and beer. Unfazed by our chutzpah, he said, 'We had a shower last night – about two inches it was. Think we might get another one today.'

We wished him well, handed him a snorkel and sped on.

As the roadworker had predicted, we were alternately drenched by rain and dried by sunshine as we rode along. The rain stung our hands, since it was too hot for gloves, but it was a good-to-be-alive kind of stinging.

You could see why the early settlers here felt as if they had arrived in the Garden of Eden. As J.G. Steele noted after talking to one of them, the bays teemed with so much mullet and snapper that you could wade out and catch them with your hands, the mangroves were stuffed solid with tasty oysters, and in their roots lived regiments of even tastier mud crabs. Stately white lilies leapt with gay abandon from the river bank, blue and white flowering vines traced their way through the jungle, kingfishers flashed through the shade and colonies of black Funereal Cockatoos flapped through the warm air like croaking umbrellas.

By lunchtime we were in Byron Bay, once the hippy capital of New South Wales until the accountants and the colonic irrigationists arrived and built five-star spas, pushing the hippies inland to Nimbin, where in fifty or so communes they still make love, smoke dope, drive ancient Beetles and Saab convertibles, and bring up children called Willow or Saffron who may or may not be theirs.

But Byron Bay is still a beautiful place, full of beautiful people. I used to know families who would drive all the way from Melbourne to spend their entire holidays here and, having seen the beaches, the scenery and the lively town for myself, it was easy to see why. The weather had improved so we had taken a drive up to the famous lighthouse, which gazes out on nothing until you hit South America, and the views there were just spectacular.

We all wanted to linger in this idyllic spot, but Brisbane (Brizzy, to us Aussies!) beckoned and we had to push on.

Several hours later, as the sun sank in a torrid sky, we rolled into Brisbane, where the Official Namer of Streets had obviously been sacked after his first two attempts, Vulture and Turbot, after which the City Council apparently christened all the streets after various English kings and queens and hired a bridge designer instead, since the eponymous river is blessed with a series of soaring arches, each one, like Fredo's pies, more breathtaking than the last.

'Song for the day?' said Matt when we stopped for the night.

'"The Banana Boat Song".'

'Weird. But appropriate.'

Pies – the most dangerous things in Australia

10

In Brisbane, we had a regular little social whirl: Matt met up with friends down the road, Colin tootled off to see an old pal in town, I went out for a Japanese dinner with my mum's cousin Fred and his daughter Deb, and in the morning John Webb, the founder of Wicked Campers, called by to say hello in his silver Porsche Carrera, the swine.

But then, he'd earned it – ten years before, he had been a mechanic who had dabbled in renting cars when he had the bright idea that if people could sleep in the vehicles they rented, they'd rent them for longer.

'To be honest, I started it for fun, and I still do it for fun; hence the rude graffiti and the turning up naked thing. If it stops being fun, and you stop having a passion for it, what's the point?' he was saying just as we were hailed from across the road by a passing old-timer.

'Oi, you don't wanna ride Triumphs, mate. AJS is the only bike,' he said, rolling up his sleeve to reveal a large AJS tattoo. 'I used to ride everywhere with me mate on ours until he went straight on at a bend and came a cropper on a barbed wire fence. Right across the neck. Nasty.'

Having thus failed his interview as head of marketing for AJS, he pottered off.

We thanked John again for the loan of Matilda and headed north. Only for her little overheating problem to crop up again in the form of a thunderous backfire which had Colin and me, following behind, almost throwing the bikes to the ground and looking for the nearest air-raid shelter.

We topped up the coolant and oil, then changed the radiator cap, but the temperature gauge was still heading north, which meant that we weren't. Still, a quick call to John, a slow and careful limp back to Brisbane's Wicked workshop, and Phil from Southend and his mate Steve were on the case. We arrived at 2.45, the radiator arrived from the nearby depot at 2.55, and they had us back on the road on the stroke of 4pm. You wouldn't get anything faster outside a Formula One pit lane.

As they were working, I wandered down the street and found a perfect example of a traditional Queensland house: cosseted by extravagant fretwork and mounted on stilts to let cool air circulate, stop floodwater doing the same and deter snakes, the little darlings.

 As Matt and I sat at the Wicked depot watching the guys sorting out Matilda's hissy fit, and with nothing else to do, I put my headline-writing skills to good use and came up with a possible code name for our Australian adventure – 'The Whiz Hard Around Oz'. Sadly I couldn't convince the other two to start calling it that, but it made me giggle all the same.

Still, Matilda's problem was sorted and she was now running cooler than she had on day one, so we were finally able to leave Brizzy. Unfortunately, our schedule had been knocked by the various delays we'd had so far so we decided not to travel to Bundaberg as originally planned, instead we made for the next stop on our itinerary, the little seaside town of Caloundra.

As we headed out of town I noticed a Queensland phenomenon – houses for sale. Of course, the fact that they were for sale was not the unusual thing, rather it was the way they were being sold. Traditional Queensland homes are raised up on stilts, so when someone wants to sell one, they just jack it up, put in on the back of a truck and send it off to a saleyard, putting a new one in its place. Then, any customer who wants to buy one will simply go along to the yard – where the houses all sit side by side on blocks – have a look around and make their choice. They then get a truck, pick up their new home and take it to their block of land where they will plonk it down again. It's a process that has more in common with the way most places sell caravans, but it's a great way to recycle fine old wooden houses that would otherwise be demolished.

The run out took us along the Bruce Highway and past the late Steve Irwin's Australia Zoo. The Crocodile Hunter still looms over the highway as a huge cut-out of his head spouts his catchphrase, 'Crikey,' while on the other side of the road another billboard features one of his kids holding a lizard and urges people to come and visit the zoo. I found the sight a bit unnerving, considering the tragic and freakish way he had died from a stingray's barb, but he is still obviously a revered character and I found the naming of a tourist scenic route after him – the Steve Irwin Way in Beerwah – much less perturbing than the giant image of his smiling face still touting for business.

It was getting on for dusk as we approached Caloundra. One minute it was twilight, the next it was dark – there is no in between at these northerly latitudes and night falls with a thud.

So with our gear safely ensconced in a motel we made our way to the bowling club down the road to sample their bangers and mash special. I know, it is a bit disturbing when you try to be a rough, tough biker and end up down at the bowling club twice in one adventure, so whatever you do, don't tell a soul.

Colin went home to bed early, and in the morning, I woke up wondering what to do about the tricky problem that, while he was brilliant at racing off to find spare radiator caps and the like, he'd only made breakfast twice so far, proving beyond doubt that he was an unreconstructed example of *Homo Australopiticus*.

After some thought, I decided there were two ways to deal with it:

1) Whack him over the head with a copy of the *Rough Guide to Australia* and say: 'Here, isn't it about time you organised the breakfast for once, you lazy Aussie drongo?'

2) Sit around waiting and whistling tunelessly.

I thought I'd go for 2) and, as usual, Colin got up, had a shower, did a bit of writing, logged on and sent all his e-mails, lay on the bed sending texts and making phone calls, went outside and had a fag, then came back in and sent some more texts. After half an hour of this, he finally cracked, and hauled out the cafetière which Gareth had donated when he left.

'Here, how do you work this bloody coffee thing?' he said.

Zen had succeeded where conflict would have failed, and perhaps it was that which led to the feeling of beautiful contentment I had as we rode up the Sunshine Coast that morning. Or perhaps it was because we had cast off our jackets and were riding in our T-shirts, feeling like boys on bicycles on our summer holidays, filled with that gloriously youthful sense of our whole lives in front of us, filled with infinite possibilities. Or perhaps it was as a result of weeks of being surrounded by people living in the endless summer that is Australia.

Whatever it was, it lasted all the livelong day, as we sped north along the section of Highway One called the Bruce Highway, with jagged blue mountains shimmering in the distance and in the foreground a vista of hills and dales, forests and streams, pine trees and palms, like the love child of Scotland and Barbados.

 We were now heading for Noosa, one of the playgrounds of the well-heeled. When I was a teenager, Noosa was where we all aspired to go for the summer and where old folks from down south went to retire. It still has a bit of that retirement community feel – a bit like I imagine Miami would be – but is a vibrant little town with a great beach, so Matt and I were able to have our first swim in the sea of the trip. As I came out of the water I noticed a woman sitting at a picnic table, laptop on and mobile phone plugged in with a Bluetooth headset. She was taking calls and working away in the shade – not a bad way to make a living. We dried off and hit the road once again, this time to put some serious miles under our belts.

Back on the Bruce Highway, we climbed up through the Great Dividing Range once again. The air was different now. Gone was the smell of eucalyptus that had accompanied us since we left the outskirts of Adelaide and all the way through the southern latitudes, only to be replaced by the more fetid, but not unpleasant, smell of jungle vegetation. The road was fabulous with banked sweeping turns that made the miles fly by.

As we drove we passed many banana, pineapple, peanut and avocado plantations, but these are actually secondary products of Queensland's industry. Instead, the area is known primarily as cattle and cane country. Cane cutters used to be as legendary as sheep shearers in Australian outback life, and some men worked as both depending on the season, travelling all over to where they were needed – it was back-breaking work. Not that it was purely a man's job. The burning of the cane to remove pests before cutting used to be an annual ritual, with women and children employed to kill the nasties as they emerged. It was part sport, part necessity and completely dangerous.

There had been violence on the cane fields too. When war took many of the men away, the growers brought in Pacific islanders known as Kanaks to do the work. Their use sparked confrontations when the local men arrived back from the war and the Kanaks were kept on as they were cheaper and less trouble.

As technology progressed however, machines replaced the cutters and the cane burners completely. All that remains now are the rusting narrow-gauge rail tracks snaking through the fields that used to carry the cut cane to the refineries. Another way of life was lost, but at least shearers still remain as there is no machine yet invented that can deal with a recalcitrant sheep.

From time to time we were stopped by the roadworks which will turn Highway One from two lanes into four, after which it will presumably be known as the Bruce and Sheila Dual Carriageway.

The great thing about bikes at roadwork queues, of course, is that you can filter all the way to the front, and this afternoon Colin set a new world record as he led the way to the front of a two-mile tailback just as the man with the 'Stop' sign swung it around to 'Slow'.

Not long after, I set a world record of my own as several beautiful but suicidal butterflies, followed by a specimen of every single bug in Queensland, flung themselves at my visor with gay abandon. Peering around the Technicolor blotches, I spied on the right at one stage a giant billboard advertising Ramada Hotels, with Mr and Mrs Perfect grinning out with perfect smiles and perfect tans after a perfect weekend break.

Unfortunately, the other side was an ad for Matilda; no, not the van, but a chain of filling stations whose mascot is a giant rabbit; who was right at the top of the billboard, so that from the other side, his giant ears looked as if they were sticking out of the top of Mr Perfect's head. Even better, just down the road was the wittiest road sign yet, saying 'Feeling Tired? Take a break. Feeling Dopey? Just keep smiling.'

Smiling as ordered, I looked at my watch and realised that it was only an hour to darkness, with still well over sixty miles to the motel in Bororen where we planned to stay the night. All too aware that this was the witching hour for Australian wildlife, we kept a careful eye out for assorted kangaroos, wombats, koalas and funnel-web spiders as, at speeds which would have had us in a Van Diemen's Land chain gang had there been any traffic cops about, we swooped and dived through lush grassland, copse and sugar plantations, on a road of such seductive curves that if it had been a woman, you would have married it and had its children, never mind the pain.

Finally, as the sun kissed the gold and azure sky farewell for another day, and as I was beginning to wonder if I had imagined the existence of Bororen, since we had not seen a single sign for it all afternoon, there was the Koorawatha Motel on our left, so sudden that we almost shot past it. We rolled up the gravel drive to its front door, laughing with happiness at the day to end all days. I got off my bike, took off my helmet, and realised that it was not quite dark after all. It had just seemed that way because of the extravagant dead insect collection on my visor.

We checked in, I gave all the insects a decent burial under the shower, and even though this was a motel in a hamlet too small to merit a signpost, Michelle the owner rustled us up succulent lamb shanks with champ and barramundi steaks, then produced an aloe vera leaf from her garden for my sunburnt hands. The colour of the nether regions of a female Savannah Baboon in the mating season, they were proof yet again that my unbending belief that I tan easily because my father is black and my mother is Italian is, in fact, a recurring delusion brought on by an overdose of Baby Disprin when I was three.

Even better, we then spent the rest of the evening amusing ourselves by picking the leaf up every time we passed it and saying, 'Allo Vera!' Apart from riding around Australia on motorbikes, you see, we don't get out much.

However, the best bit of the evening was when I was messing around with Matt's lighter and accidentally sent a tongue of flame shooting up his left nostril. Anyway, Turkish barbers charge good money for that sort of thing, and he seemed to take it well, especially when I promised I'd do the other side tomorrow for no extra charge.

Up at dawn the next morning, before long we were hurtling through Westwood, where the Sacred Heart Chapel was a corrugated iron hut smaller than my bathroom at home; and then through Comet, which according to the man at the filling station down the road was named after a sighting of one from there by an early explorer.

It was possibly the last exciting thing to happen in the town, where today the only attractions are the Fine Salami Company and the Ludwig Leichhardt Bridge, named after the Prussian explorer who arrived in Australia in 1840, and after several successful expeditions into the outback, set off from Roma near Brisbane in 1848 with seven men, fifty bullocks, two hundred and seventy goats, seven horses and several tons of supplies; none of which was ever seen or heard of again.

Unlike Colin, who having done some sterling detective work, tracked down the nearest Telstra shop located in the nearby town of Rocky, disappeared inside and emerged proudly clutching his new dongle so that we could log on wirelessly no matter where we were. It was not as impressive as my spare set, which still dangled manfully from Matilda's rear-view mirror, but it would probably be a lot more useful.

 We had a lot of distance to cover now, but thankfully the road was good – a little monotonous after the swoops and dives of the coast, but nothing compared to what we would encounter further inland. We did get some entertainment along the way from the slightly risqué billboards scattered along the highway. My favourite was one from a windscreen repair firm which carried the slogan, 'Show us your crack', which Geoff sniffily said appealed to my rough colonial humour.

We passed the lyrically named Skyring Creek, Native Companion Creek and Dry Creek, all full after the recent inundation and we motored on through Dingo – home of the Australian Dingo Trap-Throwing Championship – and the aptly-named Blackwatertown, which is the coal capital of the state and a key distribution centre. Huge freight trains, more than a kilometre long, ferry thousands of tons of coal to the ports where it is transported to China to fire their smelters to make steel – the ore for that also supplied by Australia. A lot of local people resent this arrangement as they feel they are almost giving their natural resources away, only to have to buy back the finished product which could be made at home.

Next up was Emerald city and I made sure that my 'Whiz Hard Around Oz' joke made a brief but timely reappearance as we looked for Dorothy, the Lion, the Tin Man and the Scarecrow, but they weren't there.

Emerald had been named by an early surveyor after the lush grasslands all around, and the local farmers had certainly made the most of the fertile soil, planting fields of sunflowers and groves of fruit trees, vines, lychees and rockmelons.

As we tucked into ham, cheese and tomato sandwiches, a squadron of butterflies arrived en masse and settled on Colin's bike, either because they'd never seen a Triumph before, or because they'd turned up for the funeral of their mate who'd come a cropper on his radiator.

We had ridden two hundred and fifty miles today, and would ride one hundred and fifty more before the day was out – distances which on camel or foot in the nineteenth century would have taken us weeks, months or our lives.

Leichhardt and his entire party, as I said, had never been found, and the bodies of Robert O'Hara Burke and William John Wills, who passed through this area in 1860, were only discovered after they had perished. Burke and Wills, who were to go down in history as Australia's most famous and tragic explorers, had set off from Melbourne in August that year to attempt the first south to north crossing of the unknown continent.

And if I thought I'd overpacked by bringing an extra shirt, they set out with eighteen men, twenty camels shipped with their handlers from Asia, and twenty tons of provisions, including a camel stretcher in case one of the beasts felt a touch unwell. By the time the expedition reached Cooper Creek in December, Burke had already left behind most of the men and provisions, then impatiently raced on with Wills and two other members of the party, Charley Gray and Tyrone-man John King, six camels, two horses and enough food for three months, leaving behind William Brahe to mind the camp.

Finally nearing the north coast in February 1861, they were cruelly denied the chance to reach the ocean by vast salt marshes, and turned wearily south again, their progress slowed by the wet season and increasing hunger. They killed and ate the horses and camels as their food slowly ran out, and Gray died after being beaten by Burke for stealing flour.

They finally staggered back into the Cooper Creek camp on 21 April, only to find that Brahe, after waiting an extra month for them, had left that very morning, leaving them supplies buried under a coolibah tree into which he had carved a crude sign saying 'DIG – 3 feet under'.

They trekked on, but by the time a rescue party finally found them in September, only King was still alive, Burke and Wills having died of hunger and thirst.

And if the fact that a fountain of fresh, clear water runs at the foot of the monument to them in Melbourne was not irony enough, the Leichardt Hotel across the street from us, as we polished off our sandwiches in Emerald, was advertising its Dig Tree Restaurant and ice-cold XXXX beer.

As we rode north through the dying heat of the day, I thought back to *The Dig Tree*, the late Sarah Murgatroyd's book on the Burke and Wills expedition, in which she pointed out that one of Burke's main reasons for setting out on such a dangerous expedition, apart from a desire to make his name in Melbourne society and beyond, was because he was obsessed with Julia Matthews, an actress and singer half his age.

Ah, men and their delusions of heroism again. There's nothing like dying just to prove to someone how much you want to spend the rest of your life with them.

*

By dusk we were in Alpha, a town so small it possessed only one motel and one pub, so we checked into the first and soon found ourselves in the second, tucking into food as bad as Michelle's had been good the night before.

In the silences between the clicking of the pool balls and the roar of the footie from the TV in the corner, I got talking to Danny from Kerry and his girlfriend Clare from Manchester, who were bumming around Australia and had been picking fruit for the last two months.

'Better than the last job we had, chopping the nuts off four-day-old pigs. Two hundred a day for three months. Fancy a beer?' said Clare.

On the other side of me was Ray Ladlow, a Ducati owner whose slightly better line of work was driving around collecting the sewage from septic tanks.

'You hit a load of butterflies on the road today, mate?' he said, noticing the yellow splodges all over my jacket.

'Aye, afraid so.'

'That's nothing, mate. There's a plague of giant grass-hoppers heading in from the west over the next few days. When those things hit your helmet, it's like M40 machine guns going off. Fancy a beer?' he said.

I left Colin and Matt to it and went back to the motel room to read. Which turned out to be a good decision, as Colin then got into a drinking contest with a Finnish man, downing several more pints before staggering back to the motel in the middle of the night and falling into bed.

Of course, I could have told him that getting involved in drinking with a Finn was up there with wrestling sharks in the dangerous sports league.

We'd a long run scheduled for the next day, and it looked set to be another hot one so we decided to treat ourselves to breakfast at the café where Clare said she worked. She'd offered to do us a 'full Irish' as her dad was from Donegal and she was brought up on such fare. But even though

124

Alpha only had a total of two streets, we couldn't find the café and had to settle for the local bakery instead. The guys decided on fresh apple turnovers with cream and coffees while I went for a sausage roll and tea – all good hangover food.

After a brief chat with Ray, who'd got up to see us off and to show off his modified Ducati Monster, we hit the road – though not as hard as the many kangaroos we saw dead by the road had done. The previous night's roadkill carnage was revealed in the early morning as I counted around a dozen of the poor creatures, a couple of emus, a snake and a lizard before giving up. Carrion birds were having a field day with their meals under wheels service, and even birds of prey joined in.

I surprised an enormous wedge-tailed eagle at his breakfast and was treated to the spectacle of him flying off about ten metres away from me at eye level, both of us staring at the other – me with fascination and joy, him with a cold and haughty expression.

We also passed scores of giant anthills, all facing east to west to catch the cooling effect of the prevailing winds. Darwinists will argue that this is the result of millions of years of evolution, but of course the truth is that Mr and Mrs Ant were sitting one Saturday afternoon reading *Ant Weekly* and watching the Anthill Mob on *Wacky Races* when she turned to him and said, 'Here, Anthony?'

'Yes, dear?'

'Have you ever noticed that when we're over at the Joneses' for cocktails, their place is lovely and cool, whereas ours is always like a bloody Finnish sauna? Do you think if we rebuilt this place the same way, we'd get the same effect?'

'No worries, love. I'll get onto it as soon as I've finished this fascinating article about how humans are expected to reach our level of organisation in about a million years. By the way, what's a Finnish sauna?'

The butterflies, which yesterday had all been russet with

gold and kingfisher blue spots, were today pure white and, as yet, there was no sign of Ray's killer grasshoppers.

Above the anthills and the butterflies, wedge-tailed eagles and whistling kites soared in the burning blue, descending to dine at their leisure on the dead kangaroos, emus, snakes and wallabies that had been killed in the night by passing road trains, the one-hundred-and-sixty-feet-long trucks hauling up to five containers which thunder along the highways night and day and neither stop nor swerve for man nor beast. I had already learned to turn my head to one side and duck as they swept past, bringing with them a wall of air liberally sprinkled with gravel and dust.

Day by day, the land around was looking more parched, and us with it, the only difference being that we could stop and take a slug of tepid water from a bottle in our panniers, whereas all the land could do was gaze at the occasional passing cloud above, longing for it to bequeath a blessing of rain.

11

We stopped to refuel in the small town of Barcaldine. It had been a union stronghold at one time and in 1891 saw a shearers' strike which led to the formation of the Australian Labor Party. The tree where the shearers rallied, known as the Tree of Knowledge, has been preserved under a bizarre wooden structure outside the railway station which was the focus of the dispute. The town is now home to the Australian Workers Heritage Centre, with one of the pubs called the Union Hotel. Barcaldine was also the first place where artesian water was tapped, again changing the face of the entire country, especially the outback. However, despite all that history, I didn't take to the place and it was with a sense of relief that we rode out of town.

The next little place we passed was so small we couldn't even spot a sign telling us what it was called, and it had nothing to recommend it apart from the sight of agricultural machinery of every type and size and from every era – from tractors, to ploughs, to trucks and graders – lined up on one side of the highway as it ran through town. They had all been restored and put on show, looking like a huge display of blown-up Dinky Toys; yet there was no explanation for this monument to mechanical devices, and I wondered what obsessive had put it all together, like some kind of rural art installation. I stopped to take a picture, just to prove to myself later that it was real, before again mounting up and heading on, shaking my head in disbelief.

By lunchtime we were in Longreach, the spiritual home of Qantas, as it was from here that the airline first flew. The town also markets itself as the gateway to the outback and boasts the Stockman's Hall of Fame – a tribute to the legendary cowboys of the outback and their deeds.

Many of the most famous of these were Aboriginal stock-men, who were historically paid much less than their white colleagues.

I didn't fancy going in to look at a lot of whips and saddles so Matt and I adjourned to the local Rotary Park to take advantage of its free barbecue. We cooked up some snags, wrapped them in bread with lots of tomato sauce and then had a little nap on the grass – bliss.

I had spent some time trying to persuade Colin that he really wanted to go to the Stockman's Hall of Fame so that I could bugger off to the Qantas Founders' Museum, but even the fact that it had over a hundred different types of barbed wire on display failed to stir his enthusiasm.

So while he went to sleep off his hangover in the park, I spent a happy hour pottering about the company's original 1921 hangar built by founders Hudson Fysh and Paul McGinness. The two met in the Royal Flying Corps during the First World War, with McGinness the observer picking Fysh as his pilot because he had the fewest bullet holes in his flying coat.

Several Queensland towns claim the honour of being the birthplace of Qantas, with Cloncurry's claim being that it was there that Fysh and McGinness conceived the idea; Winton's claim being that it was there that the airline was founded; and Longreach's claim being that it was here that the airline was first based before it moved to Brisbane in 1930. But my favourite version is that Fysh and McGinness came up with the idea in the bar of the Corones Hotel in Charleville, owned by the flamboyant 'Poppa' Corones, the first Greek hotelier in Australia.

What is true is that Fysh and McGinness set out to scout the area of their proposed operation in a Model T Ford, and after weeks of burst radiators, broken axles and banjaxed springs, decided that an aeroplane definitely had to be an easier way to get around, bought a second-hand Avro 504K in Sydney, and founded the Queensland and Northern Territory Aerial Service – or Qantas for short – in November 1920, which transformed the isolation of the outback.

Back then, insurers demanded to know which pilot would be flying a particular aircraft before they decided on their rate. One passenger insisted on signing his will before he left, and another took his luggage off and refused to fly at all. Mind you, they had good reason: one of the pilots, A. Vigers, noticed that his two passengers had fallen asleep and thought he'd try a quick loop. They woke at the top, were still screaming when they landed, and Vigers was fired. Another pilot, Russell Tapp, was flying a photographer over Brisbane Bay when his passenger started leaping about in the front cockpit.

'For God's sake sit down, man!' shouted Tapp.

'I can't – there's a bloody snake in the cockpit!' shouted the photographer, trying to bash the offending reptile with his camera, then losing his grip and dropping the camera into the bay. After an emergency landing, the snake was found coiled up asleep around the throttle.

Those were also the days when people generally used burning cow dung as mosquito repellent, forcing Fysh on one occasion to sleep under the billiard table in the Windorah Hotel in Western Queensland to escape the noxious fumes.

By the mid-twenties, unheard of luxury arrived in the shape of the de Havilland DH50, which seated four inside and which Qantas engineer Arthur Baird, another RFC veteran, was now able to build under licence in the hangar in which I now stood admiring one of them.

I stood there for a long time, filled with the happiness which being around old aeroplanes and motorcycles creates in me, possibly because it blesses me by osmosis with a ghost of the heroism of the men who flew and rode them, and then I got on my more modern motorcycle and rode west into the late afternoon, imagining as I did that, as well as the hum of the engine, I heard an echo of another sound, the thrumming of ancient Avros and de Havillands heading home through the dying light of the day.

And then I realised that the thrumming was coming from below me, accompanied by a staccato thudding against my boots. Looking down, I saw that they were liberally covered with bits of dead insect, and realised that Ray's grasshopper plague had come to pass. He'd just exaggerated the height they could jump.

Oh, and if you're wondering why the Corones Hotel is my favourite venue for the founding of Qantas, it's partly because Poppa Corones allegedly proposed that the airline's first planes should be named after the figures of Greek mythology, such as Hermes and Pegasus, and as a reward was granted the Qantas catering contract so that, as every plane touched down at Charleville, his staff were already on their way across the grass with food, white table linen and silver service. And even more, because when Amy Johnson stopped to refuel at Charleville during her epic flight from England to Australia in 1930, she stayed at the Corones and asked Poppa for a champagne bath to celebrate the fact that the most dangerous part of her journey was over.

Poppa duly filled a bath with sixteen bottles and, not being a man to waste a penny, not only managed to rebottle the champagne after Amy had left, but ended up with seventeen bottles, so heaven knows what Amy got up to in that bath.

Having met up with Colin and Matt, we arrived in Winton, looking forward to a Saturday night at the outdoor cinema, complete with canvas seats and original projector, only to find that it only opened on Wednesdays. Oh well, we thought, there was always the North Gregory Hotel, where 'Waltzing Matilda' was first performed in April 1895.

 The song tells the story of a swagman setting up camp and capturing a sheep to eat. When the police arrive to arrest him for the theft, which would have been a crime punishable by hanging, the worker commits suicide by drowning himself in the nearby billabong. The title comes from a colloquial term for walking (waltzing) with your possessions in your backpack (Matilda).

It was written by Banjo Patterson after he was allegedly told the tale by a local woman, Christina MacPherson, whose family home he was staying at. She then wrote the music and he put his words to it, a collaboration that caused Patterson's furious fiancé to break off their engagement.

The song has proved enduringly popular, as Aussies tend to identify with the underdog – in this case, the swagman – and it has more than once been proposed as an alternative to the national anthem. It is widely seen as the unofficial national song, instantly recognisable around the world.

Sadly, when we arrived at the hotel, it was to find that it had burnt down not once, but twice, and was now an echoing cavern whose only occupants were the owners, a tiny and pleasant Filipino woman called Vicki Simpson and her husband Jack.

'You want to see room where "Waltzing Matilda" was first sung?' said Vicki.

We followed her through the empty dining room and into an adjacent one in which the only furniture was a derelict piano.

'Is this the original piano they used for the performance?' I said hopefully.

'No. But song was sung over there,' she said, pointing at a blank wall. We stood and looked at for several seconds.

'Can't understand why no one comes to see it,' said Vicki.

'Anyway, never mind that. You want to look around bedrooms and kitchen? All very clean, very cheap.'

'No thanks. We've already got somewhere to stay,' said Matt.

'But you writers. You tell everyone how good North Gregory is, they come and stay.'

'Maybe in the morning,' I said. 'But we're leaving very early.'

'How early?'

'Maybe seven,' I lied.

'No problem. I get up at six. Knock on window, and if no answer, come around back.'

In the background, Jack pretended to dry a beer glass, pointedly gazing in the opposite direction.

Still, we decided to have dinner there anyway, eating our spaghetti bolognese while sitting on plastic chairs and watching Crocodile Dundee on all three TVs in the dining room, while the survivors of the plague of grasshoppers not killed by my boots hopped around the dance floor in the middle of the room.

The movie was singularly appropriate, since we were now approaching the part of Oz where Rod Ansell, the inspiration for Paul Hogan's character, was attacked by a crocodile in 1977 and survived in the wild for seven weeks.

He'd played down his ordeal until journalist Rachel Percy tracked him down and wrote a book on him called To Fight the Wild. Ansell ended up the chat-show circuit, Hogan saw him, and the rest is hysteria. Except for Ansell, whose plans to make something of the post-film publicity were stymied when he was banned from marketing himself as 'the real Crocodile Dundee', even though he was.

When all his cattle were shot as part of a disease-prevention scheme, Ansell lost his station and his money, was charged with assault and cattle rustling, broke up with his family and, embittered by his failure compared with the success of the film, ended up as a drug-addled recluse. In a fit of paranoia in 1999, he shot at strangers who he thought had kidnapped his son, then in the subsequent shoot-out shot a policeman dead before being gunned down himself.

By this stage we were almost wishing we were with him, since by the end of the film, Vicki had come over, by my estimation, 748 times to make absolutely certain we were going to look at her fabulously clean bathrooms and kitchens then write a rave review in *Spotless Surfaces Magazine*.

'Waltzing Matilda' is not Winton's only claim to fame – the surrounding area is also known as dinosaur country, with many fossils and tracks found in the stone on the plains around here. The nearby Lark Quarry Conservation Park has as its main exhibit the world's only recorded evidence of a dinosaur stampede. From the 3,300 fossilised footprints, palaeontologists have been able to discern that, approximately ninety-five million years ago, a large herd of small, two-legged dinosaurs was stalked by a large carnivore, and stampeded across the muddy flats to escape.

As a result, the whole town has a *Jurassic Park* meets 'Waltzing Matilda' theme to it, with statues of Patterson and his romantic swagman, and garbage bins shaped like dinosaur feet.

We rose early, tiptoed out of town and rode west. And if we'd thought the anthills of yesterday were amazing, today we were greeted by a veritable Manhattan of them: thousands of ant skyscrapers for mile after mile, and then the strangest of sights; a row of hundreds of white Brahman cattle, with their signature humps and long floppy ears, walking nose to tail across a vast field for no apparent reason.

Not to mention several sheep standing around looking nervous, as well they might, since it was not far south from here, in Blackall, that in 1892 Jackie Howe sheared 321 sheep in under eight hours by hand. It's a record that's never been broken, so someone is bound to try soon.

By now the landscape was growing increasingly bare, punctuated only by flat-topped mesas, the occasional tree and dusty side tracks leading off to farms we could not even see. What strange and lonely lives people must have lived here, and possibly still do, either by choice or destiny.

It was even worse, of course, before the days of Qantas and then the brilliant invention of the pedal-powered radio, dreamed up by the self-taught John Flynn. Working with Qantas, Flynn had set up the first Flying Doctor base in 1928 in Cloncurry, making a huge difference to the inhabitants of the isolated sheep and cattle stations of the outback, who could now not only talk to each other over the crackling ether, but know that, in an emergency, help would soon be there in the shape of a modified de Havilland DH50 whistling down to land on a hastily prepared runway.

Cloncurry, where we arrived at lunchtime, was also the site of a gold rush and extensive copper mining in the nineteenth century, but because there was no rail link to Normanton, the ore was laboriously brought out on camel trains led by Afghanis. Today, these workers lie in nameless graves facing Mecca, a few blocks from the hundred or so graves of the Chinese miners who died in terrible conditions in the gold rush. The graves are all untended and overgrown, because these men died far from those they loved and, while it is ridiculous to feel sorry for the bones which lie beneath your feet, as you stand there watching the wind blow this way and that in the grass, and the bundles of Spinifex caught on the fence glowing in the sun, it is almost impossible not to.

Mind you, perhaps they lie untended because Australians never trust anyone who doesn't drink; especially in the north, where the annual beer consumption of fifty-two gallons per man, woman and child is a world record of which the locals are understandably proud. Cloncurry's other main point of pride is that it is where the highest temperature was ever recorded in Australia – 53.1°C in January 1889 – and that was the one to which we paid most attention that day, as

Matilda's new radiator threatened to go the same way as her first.

It was, right from the start, one of those days which, as my granny always said, are sent to try you. First of all, my bike, which had been taking a while to start in the warm temperatures of the past two days, refused to start at all in Winton and had to be pushed. Still, there was a Triumph dealer three hundred miles up the road in Mount Isa, where we planned to be tonight, so I could see about that first thing in the morning.

Then Matilda began overheating, misfiring and backfiring. Suspecting dirt in the fuel because Matt had let it run low, we push-started her and told him to keep the revs up.

All was well until Cloncurry, when some idiot, possibly me, decided it would be a good idea to stop for a Magnum bar; at which point Matilda's battery died and she stopped completely. Another push, and she was off, only for the same thing to happen a few minutes down the road, then again after another push, by which time we were soaked with sweat in the searing heat.

Closer examination by Colin revealed that the battery was either dead or not charging, the radiator header tank had come loose and been holed by the fan, and the engine was only firing on two of its four cylinders. Gaffer tape failed to seal the hole in the tank, and we stood around scratching our heads.

'What about sticking a plastic bag inside it to act as a membrane?' I said, making my only practical contribution to the expedition, or possibly ever. At first that seemed to work, but five minutes later, everything stopped again, this time for good.

It was now only a couple of hours to dark, and we were stranded in the middle of nowhere. Still, one thing adventures teach you is that there's always a solution, and after a speculative walk up the hill, Colin got a signal on his phone, called John and got the number of RACQ, the breakdown service Wicked used.

We called them, and forty-five minutes later, mechanic

Barry Woodhouse was there with his tow truck, as helpful and cheery as everyone else in Australia, in spite of the fact that we'd dragged him away from the footie. Half an hour after that, we were back in Cloncurry with Matilda booked into the local garage for first thing in the morning, and us booked into the Wagon Wheel Motel, in whose dining room we had to make do with lamb shanks and Moroccan chicken tagine with jasmine rice and toasted almonds. Bush tucker? What bush tucker!?

Next morning, I spent more time rescuing suicidal insects from the shower than actually showering. One particularly stupid grasshopper actually leaped back in twice before I finally rescued him, dried him out with the aid of some toilet roll and sent him hopping away. It was the least I could do, after killing all his mates on the road the day before.

The word on Matilda, meanwhile, was that she just needed a new battery, header tank and alternator, which we could get up the road in Mount Isa, so while the mechanic got working, I rode on to Mount Isa to see if I could get the Triumph's starting problem sorted.

On the way, I passed the ghostly remains of Mary Kathleen, the town built in 1956 around the site where a local couple were wandering around after their car broke down and found uranium ore. When the anti-nuclear lobby stopped exports in 1982, the town was completely dismantled, and now only the shadowy outlines of front drives and lawns mark where a thriving community once stood.

I got back on the bike, which I'd left running just in case, and half an hour later was standing in Mount Isa Motorcycles.

'You the blokes riding two Tigers around Oz?' said Joy at the front desk. 'Well, we don't do Triumphs any more, but Mark here will see what he can do.'

'Mmm, the battery's not charging properly, so looks like the stator and rectifier aren't working. You can get it sorted out at the Triumph dealer in Darwin, but I'll give it a charge to get you that far,' said Mark, then didn't charge me a cent.

I bought a set of jump leads with the money he'd saved me, and found a disturbingly expensive motel, which then wiped out any savings I'd made for the day.

Meanwhile, Matt and I had been hanging about in Cloncurry waiting for Matilda to come back to life. We headed back to the motel and passed the time by doing some work, but in only two hours the van was ready to go, and we set off for Isa.

As we drove we passed several birds of prey quartering the road. There was one at least every kilometre, gliding in the breeze, looking for prey or roadkill. They were similar in build to a large hawk, with a wingspan of about three feet and were beautiful to see as they hung in the air just metres above us, occasionally peeling away, frightened by the sound of the engines.

The road seems to be a lifeline for them as it supplies food and also thermals for them to soar on as the heat rises from the tarmac. In the course of the past two days we had seen more of these wild hunters than you would see of any types of birds of prey in a lifetime in Europe. I'd asked the locals what they were but they just shrugged – the birds were just part of the scenery.

And this scenery was pretty spectacular – ancient escarpments of red rock that told you this was the Australian outback and nowhere else in the world, while the whole area was dotted with anthills the same colour as the soil, standing like stalagmites everywhere you looked, some in the most bizarre shapes and as tall as a person. The road climbed up and down through the rocky outcrops, past abandoned mines and ghost towns, with hardly another car on the road.

It was easy to imagine dinosaurs roaming this land millions of years ago.

It was hot too, thirty-five degrees at least, and by the time we saw the tall chimneys of Isa, we were both parched. We left Matilda at the auto-spark's for the night, then Matt and I went to the Telstra shop to try and get our dongle sorted out. We hadn't been able to get it to work since we bought it in Rocky and, as Geoff can attest, there is nothing worse than non-functioning dongles.

I had been driven to near insanity trying to get assistance from the Telstra helpline, which is one of the biggest misnomers in the history of telecommunications. At the shop we were given some software, but only after we had to buy a brand-new memory stick to ensure we did not introduce any nasty viruses to their system. We brought it back to the motel that Geoff had booked for us, only to find that it still didn't work.

That evening, riding through the sultry heat to pick up some supplies for breakfast and a few beers to go with our takeaway fish and chips, I was suddenly struck with an intense memory of the smell of California, where I had lived and played volleyball in my twenties.

It was an aroma so intangible I can hardly describe it other than the sun on warm skin, coconut oil and under it all the salty tang of the Pacific; which was surprising, since I was riding through a mining town full of slag heaps, giant yellow trucks and even more giant chimneys, which was at least a thousand miles from the nearest ocean.

'Song for the day?' said Matt as I arrived back all the way from California with the beer.

'"What a Wonderful World", by Louis Armstrong.'

'Touching optimism, with a hint of naiveté,' he said, popping a tinny.

The next morning, the word on Matilda was that her alternator seemed to be working, and that the battery was charged up and ready to go. Naturally, five minutes up the road, the battery light came on, and Matt stopped, a worried look on his face.

'Do you want to go back to the garage?' said Colin.

'No point. They'd just tell us she was all right when she left them, the way Belfast people say about the *Titanic*,' said Matt.

'Anyway, the battery light was on for the past five weeks out of Adelaide, so she should make it the four days to Darwin,' I said.

Matt drove on, and we followed in Kierkegaardian fear and trembling, our hearts slowly lifting with every passing mile until we stopped two hours later to refuel at the roadhouse at Camooweal, of which the guidebook had said, 'The township's atmosphere of lazy aggression is exacerbated by a total lack of charm.'

They must have hit it on a bad day, for the mother and daughter who ran the roadhouse couldn't have been more friendly.

'Here, is everyone blonde and gorgeous around here?' I said to the mum as I paid for the fuel.

'All except him,' she said, tilting her head towards a swarthy young man working in the kitchen.

'I'd be worried if he found me blonde and gorgeous,' he grinned.

'So would I,' I said.

Our bad-luck streak hadn't quite run out though as, just out of town, Matt was pulled over by the police for driving too close to Geoff. I chucked a uey to have a word as Matt pulled away, and the cop, who was actually pretty friendly, said, 'I just thought he was driving too close to your mate, and didn't know you were all travelling together, no worries mate.'

After driving along the same dead-straight road for another 80km, Geoff and I were pulled over outside a police station in the middle of nowhere – the same cop we had encountered earlier was now doing random breath tests. We reckoned that he and his partner were just bored and wanted to have a look at the bikes, and sure enough, one of them turned out to be a biker.

After they had breathalysed us, and Geoff revealed he had left his licence at home – 'It's okay, too much paperwork, mate' – we had a yarn about what we were up to and they told us that the next bend was 480 kilometres away.

'We'll have to be re-trained,' I said

'No worries. Once you turn right there, there's another couple of bends before Darwin – you'll love it, it's really interesting bike country.'

Leaving them laughing, we set off in pursuit of Matt – only another 280 kilometres of flat, dead-straight road before our next stop with the heat shimmer inducing drowsiness and only the whistling kites – as I'd finally found out the birds of prey were called – for company.

The heat was intense, and even at 70 or 80mph, the wind was like a hairdryer set to maximum, with no discernible cooling effect. It played tricks on your vision as well; I kept thinking I saw Matilda ahead, then it would turn out to be a tree, or a road train coming the other way.

Of Matilda, though, there was no sign, so Matt had either swerved off the road and been eaten, van and all, by starving kangaroos, or he had refuelled her on avgas. Finally we saw him through the shimmering haze, and as we drew closer he gave a cheery wave, in the manner of bomber pilots returning from Germany when they saw their fighter escort.

'We have you in sight, M for Matilda.'

'Good to see you, little friends.'

'Break left, Blue Two! Wombats at six o'clock!'

'That's all right, Red Leader, it's only half past five.'

Sadly, what Blue Two had failed to realise was that, having crossed the border from Queensland into the Northern Territory and a new time zone, half five was now six. In any case, it was nearly dark, and how glad we were as Barkly Homestead swam into view, for it was the only place to stay, drink or eat for hundreds of miles.

Even the fact that the roadhouse had no rooms left and we had to sleep in Matilda at the campsite around the back failed to dampen our gratitude at having got there. And anyway, the owner swore that the food was the best for miles around.

Having lost half an hour, I then proceeded to lose my glasses, and spent a fruitless hour wandering aimlessly around the campsite, asking the homestead owner if she'd seen them, tearing the van apart and interrogating a number of large beetles, since they looked as if they needed glasses from their habit of walking into walls, scratching their heads then wandering off in an entirely different direction.

At last Colin, using all the bush skills he had learned from several years living in north Belfast, found them exactly where I'd left them. Still, at least two good things came out of it – it gave me a major victory in the Poggle Wars, and I found the jar of fine marmalade which I'd bought three weeks before, and which Matt had contrived to lose within fifteen seconds somewhere in the chaos he called his 'filing system' in the back of the van.

After a hearty supper, Colin went to sleep on a mattress under the awning of the caravan next door and I tried in vain to do the same, since Matt and I were sleeping head to tail in the back of Matilda and he spent the entire night trying to shove his big toe up my nose.

Yawning mightily as we set off up the road the following morning, I was only saved from nodding off and veering into a nearby eucalyptus when after an hour and a half the excitement suddenly reached fever pitch in the shape of a corner. A long, sweeping left-hander, but a corner just the same. Fortunately, the traffic cops the day before had warned us about it, so we were ready for it, even if it did take all our strength to wrestle the handlebars from the straight ahead position they had seized in.

And just when we thought things couldn't get any better, the Three Ways junction appeared. We stopped, checked carefully that our maps were the correct way up, and turned right, since left would have led us to Alice Springs and the short way to Adelaide, rather than Darwin and down the west coast.

To relieve the boredom of the endless straights, Colin and I finally decided to put them to some use by having a race, and as we were hurtling along side by side at a shade over 130mph, the thought suddenly occurred to me that this was only the average speed of the Isle of Man TT lap record set by John McGuinness the year before on winding country roads.

It was about time we slowed down anyway, since a wind had sprung up from nowhere, flinging us this way and that across the road, and we found the reason why when we stopped to refuel; a sign in the window of the filling station saying, 'Fishing contest cancelled due to cyclone'.

'You're lucky. Today's just the end of it,' said the woman behind the counter.

Later that day we stopped at a town called Elliott. We had considered staying there, but decided against it after realising it was a prohibited area, with no alcohol allowed and no fuel, as it is a mainly Aboriginal town. The idea is to try and stop petrol-sniffing and drinking and provide a safe haven for families, many of whom were sitting in groups under the trees in the main street. The children were curious about the bikes but the adults all looked pretty glum and not too friendly, which is understandable as white people and society haven't exactly treated them too well overall.

The old attitudes have changed quite a bit over the past few years, but not as much or as quickly as they should have. I found it sad to see these people, who have lost most of their own rich culture and have gained nothing from ours, remaining fringe-dwellers on the edge of modern Australian society, living in a kind of limbo, with little hope of change in their lifetime.

There is a severe unemployment problem among the Aboriginal people since the government introduced equal pay rules a decade or so ago in a misguided attempt to improve their lot. As a result, many unscrupulous employers simply let their Aboriginal employees go, causing whole communities to leave the various stations and homesteads they had worked and lived on and head into town where they have few options but to eke out an existence surviving on government handouts. Koorie people are more likely to die from suicide, die younger and develop diseases that most white people will never have to worry about.

It was with a sombre outlook and a heavy heart that we mounted our bikes and pushed on towards Daly Waters.

Colin at termite metropolis

12

The Daly Waters Pub is a place I had always wanted to see ever since I was a kid and had first read about it in *Australasian Post*, that same magazine that featured the Ettamogah Pub cartoons. It is one of those quirky outback pubs, where people leave all kinds of souvenirs to show they've been there.

There are flags and football scarves from all over the world, currency from every nation you can think of, and a few you can't, but most interesting is the collection of women's bras, signed by their owners, that festoon the bar. There is also a helicopter on the roof of an outbuilding and all sorts of other bits and pieces scattered around, from chairs made out of barrels to a joke parking meter out the front – all this in a town which is basically the pub and a few rooms and cabins run by the owner. We got a room from the German girl behind the bar which turned out to have décor à la *Prisoner Cell Block H*, with walls that wobbled just as much, and settled in.

Daly Waters held significance for me too, as it was through this town that John McDouall Stuart had passed on his successful journey from Adelaide to Darwin. Stuart was born in Fifeshire in 1815, graduated as a civil engineer, and in 1838 called around to ask his fiancée if she would emigrate to Australia with him. Only to round the corner and, to his horror, see her in the arms of her cousin, his friend William Russell.

Not realising that Russell was also leaving for Australia and was just giving his cousin a platonic hug, the heartbroken Stuart sailed for Adelaide the next day. And although he never spoke of his broken engagement again, the pain of it stayed with him for ever, and he would go for months without a drink then lock himself in a room and get stuck into a bottle of whisky with a vengeance.

Shunning society and the company of women, the independent, solitary figure became a legendary explorer who succeeded where others such as Leichhardt and Burke and Wills had failed by eschewing large, cumbersome parties in favour of small, mobile expeditions. He would probably have approved of motorbike adventures, I thought, as I stood looking at the 'S' which he had carved into a tree as he passed this way on 23 May 1862.

Four years earlier, he had been exploring south of here when he came upon a native who gazed at him with a mixture of astonishment and fear, then leaped into a nearby Mulga bush imagining that that would save him, in the same way that snow leopards apparently imagine themselves invisible from predators if they place their paw over their eyes; a quaint but misguided delusion which is possibly one of the reasons snow leopards are dying out.

By all accounts, both Stuart and the women who had left their underwear pinned to the wall of the pub had had a better time in Daly Waters than the wartime airmen based down the road at the aerodrome.

This had opened as a civil airfield in 1928 and, according to the airfield cook, secretary and general factotum Henriette Pearce, Lady Mountbatten was among the first passengers through it.

'No one knew until she'd gone,' wrote Henriette in her

diary. 'In those days, the highlight of the morning was the arrival just before eight of the planes from Queensland, Singapore and Perth. They'd come wheeling in from three different directions, circle and all be on the ground by one minute to eight, and we had twenty minutes to get them refuelled, fed and out again, so by a quarter to eight, I'd have eggs boiling in a colander and the tea on, and when passengers landed, for breakfast they could have homemade bread, eggs, hot scones, a variety of cakes, honey on the comb, tea and coffee.'

Ah, if only Henriette had been around during the war to brighten up the lives of men like Fitter Murry Lawson, who said, 'Daly Waters was the pits. The bore water smelt so bad that not even tea could disguise it'; and pilot Bob Dalken, who said, 'It was appalling. The flies were out of this world. If you did have a mosquito net, you'd wake up hardly able to see out because of the mass of flies on it waiting for you to get up.'

It was a half-mile trudge to the showers, and men arrived back as dirty as when they'd set out. When the Americans arrived in 1942, Lt Albert Spehr attempted to impress the locals with a slow roll over the airfield. Duly impressed, they all turned up for his funeral the next day after he got it slightly wrong and spun into the ground.

The next year, a squadron of Spitfires was based there and, after the war, the airfield returned to civil use until it was closed in 1971, after which Daly Waters became a ghost town. Filled with the ghosts of women who have lost their underwear, that is.

Of the Spitfires, all that remains is a rusting Merlin engine up the road at the little museum in Larrimah which, from the look of it, suffered an even bigger overheating problem than Matilda. And as for the aerodrome, all that remains today is the wind whistling through Hangar No. 5 the rusting remains of an Avro Anson in the long grass beside the runway, and the corrugated iron officers' mess, slowly sinking into the entropy of the bush.

I arrived back at the pub to find that, although it had been empty when we arrived – except for a gnarled bushman in the regulation blue singlet, faded shorts and Blundstone boots – every single backpacker in the world had now turned up in what looked like an attempt to set a world beer-drinking record.

In the circumstances, it seemed impolite not to join them, and although I gave up at ten o'clock and went to bed, Colin remained until four in the morning, at which stage I dimly heard him crawl into bed muttering that his head was hurting.

'Try tying a piece of string around it. That's what Ludwig Leichhardt did when one of his men got a headache,' I muttered darkly.

'Did it work?'

'No, but it gave them all a laugh.'

He was still fast asleep the next morning when I got up at seven, and I was standing at the loo just about to have a pee when I noticed a large green frog looking up at me from the bowl. As I bent to scoop him out, he disappeared up the U-bend, and as I was emerging after relieving myself behind some nearby bushes instead, I ran into the owner of the premises.

'Here, do you know you've got a frog in your bog?' I said.

'Oh yeah, we've loads of them. They can get out, but they seem to like it there,' she said.

Back at Matilda, I found Matt making breakfast and, as we sat tucking into coffee and toast, he said, 'You know, I haven't seen a single bloody live kangaroo the whole trip, and I'm going home in a few days. I think they're made up by the tourist board just to attract gullible folk like us.'

Just then, a large, strangely familiar brown animal hopped by about twenty yards behind him.

'Turn around, Mattie. Right now,' I said.

He did, and was smiling all morning until the moment we were sitting at a random police checkpoint when Matilda's engine suddenly coughed, spluttered and expired.

'Battery,' said Matt grimly as the nearest policeman came over, looked in the window, then drove his patrol car over and gave us a start with my new jump leads. In Australia, even the police are on Prozac.

By early afternoon we were pulling into Katherine, and although my wife's version of the name is spelt with a C, it still did strange things to my heart. On my finger I wore her ring, engraved with the Viking rune for joy, light and new beginnings, and every morning before I set out, as I had on the long road from Chile to Alaska four years before, I checked in my pocket to make sure that the little box of silver good-luck charms she had given me then was safe and sound.

These were only little things, but they kept hope one step ahead of despair, as did the disturbingly few things I had learnt in life – that it is not what happens to you, but how you react to it that makes the difference; that regretting the past and worrying about the future simply ruins the present; and that we have a choice when we wake up every morning to be happy rather than miserable, to look for the good rather than seek out the bad, and to do good with every little act of our day.

We rode down the only street, which in 1998 was two-metres deep in water after a cyclone which left crocodiles cruising lazily past Woolworth's, but today there was neither a cloud in the sky nor a croc in the street, so using a combination of the native bush skills I had picked up and a credit card, I bought supplies for lunch.

We were tucking into ham and cheese sandwiches, that staple for adventurers, in the park across the road when from the adjoining caravan emerged a small man, a large woman and a tiny dog, all equally cheery. They turned out to be Rod, Heather and Teeny, two 'grey nomads' and their matching pooch who had sold their house, taken early retirement and now spent their time travelling around Oz.

'Got to get some grog,' said Rod. 'I make me own ginger beer, see? Great stuff: 16 per cent, and no hangover, but we met a couple of German cyclists called Bruno and Eva last night and we polished off my last batch. Shame, because it was made with Barcaldine water, pure as snow, comes from thousands of feet underground. Now I have to wait a week before the next lot's ready.'

And with that, he pottered across the road, keeping a careful lookout for crocodiles.

Several miles down the road an intriguing sign for a pub called the Pink Panther, advertising a 'Free Zoo' caused us to halt for a break. It was another outback pub full of character with its own museum and a melted Spitfire engine on show. It had cages full of native birds and animals and all its cabins were painted a hot pink. We deduced that there must have been an offer on the paint as there was no other obvious connection with the movies or cartoon character, save the barman's slight resemblance to Inspector Clouseau.

We happened to arrive at the same time as a tour party made up of teenage Americans and Germans which proved fortuitous, as their guide led us all out to watch a small saltwater crocodile known as 'Sneaky Sam' being fed. The guide used a rod to dangle pieces of chicken over the pool and the croc leapt up and snapped them off.

I went inside the enclosure to see close up, protected only by a length of fence open at either end, Matt came in to film but Geoff bravely stayed outside surrounded by teenage girls that he could throw at the croc should it decide to sample some Tyrone cuisine. That may have been a wise move, however, as the guide informed us that Sam had killed his last girlfriend, a crocodile that was bigger than him. Perhaps some kind of charity needs to be set up to protect female crocs, as there's obviously some deep-rooted anger issues there among the males.

A small town called Pine Creek was our next destination as I had booked us in to what turned out to be a fairly ropey Portakabin on a caravan park. It was no more than a former shipping container lined with brown Formica and with a lawn sprinkler outside, which meant sprinting across the grass to the front door to avoid getting soaked. Its only saving graces were a fridge and air conditioning.

Still, the food in the pub across the road was good, and the local freesheet, *Up The Creek*, was entertaining in a car crash kind of way. The title reminded me of our own predicament as we had come to realise that at the rate we were spending, with the exchange rate dropping and the price of fuel going up the more remote we got, we'd be the first expedition to push two motorcycles across the Nullarbor Desert.

Colin opted for an early night so, leaving him snoring like a baby warthog, Matt and I wandered back to the pub across the road in the lilac dusk when from the north there came a great whispering, and above our heads swept giant fruit bats on their way home to roost for the night.

We stood for a good twenty minutes as they streamed overhead, until at last there was silence. Followed a few minutes later by a muffled crash as in the eucalyptus woods to the south, an unfortunate tree collapsed under the weight of several thousand bats.

As I did later myself: stepping out onto the lawn in the middle of the night to answer a call of nature, I tripped on the step and fell full length on the grass. Whereupon the sprinkler leapt into action. Stark naked and dripping, I ran into the bushes, had a pee, then ran back across the grass and hauled on the door of the room. It refused to budge, no matter how much I pulled and tugged at it. It was only after five minutes of cursing, swearing and being sprinkled on that I realised it opened inwards.

'Song for the day?' said Matt as we nodded off in our deluxe shipping container.

'A medley from *The Very Best of Cat Stevens*; "Moonshadow", "Tea for the Tillerman" and "Hard Headed Woman".'

'Obvious yearnings for lost youth,' he said, and went to sleep.

In the morning, after a hearty breakfast of juice, raw toast with fine marmalade and coffee brewed up on our little stove, we were off for the last run into Darwin, the furthest north we would get, and the turning point of the trip, both geographically and emotionally, in the same way as Cartagena on the north coast of Colombia had been four years earlier.

This time, it would mark the halfway point of the journey, and also the farewell to Matt, which was a shame, since he had now achieved black-belt status in the twin arts of sandwich making and Matilda tending, which his replacement Paul would now have to start learning from scratch.

 Of course being the rugged adventurers we knew ourselves to be, we were not going to let ourselves get emotional, and instead focused on the fact that our run into Darwin was expected to be fairly straightforward. Our main worry was that we were making the journey on Good Friday, the only day in the year that the pubs closed, allowing hotel workers to have a guranteed day off.

As a student working pubs, I had looked forward to the day as the hotel owners held and paid for an annual barbie which usually ended up a very messy event with people being slung into rivers and so on. It was basically a delayed Christmas party, with the usual recriminations later as people over-indulged and got stuck into the boss, or each other, in every way you could think of.

We push-started Matilda after breakfast, and Matt sped on, followed by Colin and I under a full moon which had still not gone to bed from the night before, and through groves of eucalyptus, palm and pine punctuated by termite mounds which made the ant metropolis of a few days ago seem like mud huts.

If the anthills had been Manhattan, this was the Dubai of the insect world, and if you looked hard enough, you could almost see termites at the top of each one toiling away in little djellabahs and hard hats, while in air-conditioned tunnels far below, others wearing eye shades and sleeve clips were putting the finishing touches to advertisments in *Termite Times* saying, 'Invest now in Termite Towers! World's highest apartments at 25ft! Fabulous views of, er, well, other termite mounds.'

From time to time, too, we would pass some of the fifty Second World War airfields which had been built here after the Japanese bombed Darwin in February 1942; initially as a series of fall-back defence outposts in case the Japanese invaded, and then when that failed to happen, as bases to attack Japanese forces in East Timor and the Philippines for the rest of the war. Several of them, such as Strauss, Sattler, Livingstone and Hughes, still run alongside the road, so that you can almost hear Spitfires burbling in over the threshold.

We stopped to look at a war graves cemetery at the small Adelaide River settlement and, as I rode in I disturbed a kangaroo enjoying a late breakfast on the neat lawns along the Avenue of Honour. It shot out in front of me and I missed it by a few feet, not that I had any choice in the matter as it was there and gone before I'd had any time to react. It was a timely reminder of just how dangerous our friend Skippy could be to innocent bikers out for a morning tootle.

Glad both of us were okay, I went on to the cemetery, which was bigger than expected and lovingly maintained by the Australian War Graves Association. There were rows of simple plaques to all of the fallen, each with an individual message from their families. Some were religious, some personal, some simple but heartfelt, with one from a widow to her husband who was just twenty years old when he died, the plaque simply read, 'Jim'.

The RAAF seemed to have borne the brunt of the Japanese assault judging by the number of its peronnel here, but there were also soldiers, sailors, merchant marines and, just to show there was no colour bar, two obviously Chinese men who were serving as cooks when they met their fate serving their adopted homeland.

We were quite affected by the whole spectacle of so many young men killed in their prime, and we reflected on the futility of war, especially as Geoff and I have both witnessed the effects as reporters in Ireland and, in my case, further afield. It was a stark reminder of just how close Australia had come to being invaded by the Japanese, and how different things could have been.

At one stage I pulled alongside Colin and shouted across, 'Excuse me, is this the road to Darwin?'

'I think so!' he yelled.

'Thanks. Nice bike.'

He grinned, and sped on, and before long we were trying to get accustomed to sights we had not seen for a week and a half, like street lights, traffic lights and, indeed, traffic, as at last we rolled into Darwin which was, until the First World War, the most dissolute, exotic and isolated town in Australia.

The inhabitants, according to historian Phillip Knightley, had been an eclectic medley of Aussies, Greeks, Chinese, Malays, Scandinavians, Russians, Syrians, Patagonians, Turks, Afghanis, Japanese and Italians. At that time there had been no air service, no road and no railway, and it took two weeks to get there by sea from Sydney; pretty much the same time we had taken by road, I thought as we arrived.

Matilda, having given her all, finally died and coasted into the Wicked depot yard with a dead battery just as the heavens opened with the tropical downpour to end all downpours. It seemed appropriate, for in the wet season here blinding rainstorms are so regular that work becomes impossible and drinking the only alternative.

One visitor in 1911, encountering yet another sozzled local stumbling along a muddy street lined with rubbish, described the town as 'the most squalid and contemptible place I ever saw'.

Later that year, the government, determined to put an end to this depravity, sent in the authoritarian Scot Dr John Gilruth who, within a year, made himself the most hated man in the Northern Territory with a series of draconian laws which formed part of his masterplan to find a British investor to buy the Territory from the Australian Government and appoint him Grand Viceroy.

If it sounds daft, it almost succeeded with the help of the incredibly wealthy Vestey brothers of Liverpool, William and Edmund, who owned cattle stations all over the world, and who rented four million acres of the Territory for a piffling annual rent of £1,650, then spent £1 million on a huge abattoir in Darwin which they opened in 1917 and closed in 1920, blaming 'labour indiscipline'.

It may have been the truth, for they had the militant trade unionist Harold Nelson to cope with, but it could also have been the greatest scam of all time, in that by building the slaughterhouse then not running it, the Vesteys ensured that no one else would move in, and that Australian beef would not compete with their South American interests.

Today, all that is left of that £1 million investment is the most expensive patch of wasteland in the world.

As if virtual meat plants and the union riots which followed the closure of the abattoir weren't bad enough, Darwin was then bombed by the Japanese five days after Singapore fell in February 1942, destroying twenty-three ships and sending a locomotive, which had been deck cargo on one merchantman, sailing through the air past astonished onlookers.

The raid was so unexpected that when Sgt W.J.F. McDonald of the machine gun battalion based on the northern headland phoned Captain H. Brown in Darwin to report Japanese planes overhead, Brown said, 'Mac, I'm busy. Don't play games with me. How do you know they're Japs?'

'Because they've got bloody great red spots on them,' was McDonald's memorable reply.

After the raid, and another two years later, a wave of panic that invasion was imminent swept through the city and led to a day of shame which has haunted Darwin to this day. Men tried to force their way onto an evacuation train for women and children and, when an air-raid siren sounded and everyone took cover, the train crew abandoned them and headed south at full speed.

Most civilians fled the city, leaving the army to maintain order; only for the soldiers to stop civilians looting by the unusual expedient of doing it themselves. They stripped the Qantas freight office, holding staff at bay with a broken bottle; they looted homes and offices; they stole cars; and most shamefully of all, they thieved the possessions of nurses working around the clock in the military hospital, then commandeered a freighter and shipped all their stolen spoils to their friends and families on the south coast.

It was not Darwin's finest hour, and both the bombing and the subsequent looting was covered up by the government for the rest of the war. In fact, the only person who seems to have kept his head throughout the sorry affair was a Greek businessman who stood beside the road as hordes of soldiers and civilians fled south in commandeered vehicles offering cash to anyone who would sell their home for a song. Most did, and he made a packet.

The true heroes of the hour, though, were the ten US Army Air Corps pilots who, in outdated Kittyhawks, took on 188 Japanese aircraft on the morning of the raid, knowing that they faced almost certain death. Only one plane and four pilots survived, and the Purple Heart of one who didn't, Lt Jack Peres, is on display in the Aviation Heritage Museum up the road, only yards away from the Japanese Zero which Hajime Toyoshima crash-landed the same morning after being hit. Toyoshima was disarmed and captured by Aboriginals, who then took him to Bathurst Island and handed him over to Sgt Leslie J. Powell who, using Toyoshima's own service pistol, escorted him into captivity. He was later to die in the breakout of Japanese prisoners from the Cowra POW camp in August 1944.

I looked at his photograph and then that of Jack Peres, both of them eager and smiling on the day they qualified as pilots, and thought of the war graves we had seen back down the road, of men who had died in their late teens and early twenties, each with heartbreaking inscriptions like, 'From your loving wife Thelma, who will never forget you. A link has been broken that will never be repaired.'

It is all too easy to think that war is exciting and glamorous, but the truth is that all it does is kill people, leaving those behind looking at an empty seat by the fire for the rest of their lives. Oh well, at least the closest I'll ever get to it is shooting down Messerchmitts on the flight simulator in the study, I thought, getting on the bike and riding back into a city which after having most of its old buildings bombed by the Japanese, then had the rest destroyed by Cyclone Tracy on Christmas Eve 1974.

Two hundred people lost their lives the night that the cyclone struck, a huge amount given the size of the population, with many more injured and the entire city almost flattened. I was just a kid at the time, and hadn't been in the country that long but I remember the scenes on the television.

It looked like a nuclear warhead had hit the city, and the sight of refugees landing in the other capitals, including Melbourne, was heart-rending. People filed off the cavernous military aircraft with just the clothes they stood up in, obviously still numb with shock. The rest of the country rallied around to help, just as it did during the aftermath of the bushfires in Victoria in 2009, and people donated clothes and toys for the children who had lost everything.

Even as a child, the impact of the tragedy was not lost on me, probably because the cyclone came at that most important time of the year for children, and I tried to imagine what it would have been like to go to bed on Christmas Eve expecting to get up and open all your presents, only to have that kind of terror descend upon you. Perhaps because we had experienced upheaval ourselves it affected me more than most and I remember donating some chocolate to the relief effort – no greater sacrifice in my eyes as I had a very sweet tooth in those days.

A girl whose family fled the aftermath of the cyclone actually ended up being placed at my school and I quizzed her all about it, just as others had quizzed me about the Troubles in Belfast, and listened wide-eyed to her recollections. Her family never went back to Darwin – many refugees didn't – scared that it would all happen again.

Those Darwinians who did return collected all the stones and rebuilt what they could, including Government House and the old courthouse and jail, whose original opening in 1884 was greeted with the following stirring words of Thomas Kennedy Pater, editor of *The North Australian*.

> The new courthouse was opened on Tuesday last without any ceremony whatever, except that of trying a man for cattle stealing. The interior of the building is pleasing enough, but we cannot say that the view of it from the street is suggestive of anything other than a grocer's shop. The cells we did not inspect – but are likely to do at any time.

Indeed, it looked as if we'd be glad of a nice cosy cell before long ourselves for, after checking our finances, we discovered that a collapsing exchange rate meant that they were looking even worse than ever, with a budget of about fifty quid a day each for the rest of the trip, which meant that even if we stayed in shipping containers and rode at 20mph to save fuel, we'd have no money left for things like food.

'Well, we'll all be dead in fifty years, and none of this will matter. All those in favour of ignoring the problem and having a beer say "Aye",' I said.

'Aye,' said Colin.

'Aye,' said Matt, who didn't care because he was going home in two days anyway and being replaced by Paul.

In any case, by having a beer we were just supporting the statistic that Darwin's alcohol consumption is 50 per cent higher than the national average, with a matching murder rate, mostly because there's nothing else to do in the wet season than drink then start a fight. It's hardly surprising, because even though we'd arrived at the end of it, the air was still so humid that the moment you walked out the door, your sunglasses misted up so that you ended up stumbling into lampposts while grannies came up, took you gently by the arm and asked if you realised that your guide dog had run away.

Still, it could have been worse. The news from home was that Ireland was under three feet of snow, and that three hundred people had been trapped in an ice storm on the Glenshane Pass after ignoring warnings not to drive. Silly buggers. They're the sort of people who set out across the outback in a dodgy van, and deserve all they get, if you ask me.

Talking of dodgy vans, the news from the Wicked depot was that they had ordered the wrong alternator, thus wasting another day to add to the long weekend over Easter. Even worse, they had spoiled us by lending us a smooth diesel van with a piffling two hundred thousand kilometres on the clock, but our increasingly unsubtle hints to them that they could give us that for the second half of the trip had landed on deaf ears, then fallen on stony ground.

Colin communes with Skippy

13

Darwin seemed to be the hedonistic capital of Australia. It was so hot and humid that most people seemed to spend their lives lounging around the pool, at the pub or in air-conditioned coffee shops.

Most of the young people staying at our backpackers' hostel worked various jobs, though how anyone worked in that heat was beyond us. The rest of the time they were hanging out somewhere cool, and in the evenings the streets were full of people carousing until the early hours. It was definitely a city for the young.

One woman who had been living there for over thirty-five years told us, 'When we came here no kids had grandparents living here, and if you had them you were considered very lucky. Now we are grandparents but most people move up here when they are young. Some stay, but most eventually leave as the climate gets to them in the end.'

The climate was pretty stifling and we were keen to move on, but, thanks to the difficulties we were having with Matilda, we had several days of waiting stretching in front of us. Still, it was a good chance to rest up and get our washing done, though drying stuff in that humidity was a challenge.

By Easter Sunday Paul, the new cameraman, had arrived so

we spent the day exploring Darwin. By the time we had returned to our room, we were all drenched with sweat and looked like extras from *Apocalypse Now* or *Platoon*. We collapsed onto our beds in our blessedly cool room and wondered how anybody could walk about in this heat. It must take years to acclimatise to this and it was easy to see how people 'go troppo' in the heat – and, by all accounts, we were there at the start of the cool season.

After four days of waiting around, we were all keen to get back out on the road as cabin fever and a kind of torpor had started to set in. Paul especially wanted to get out amongst it, as all he had seen since he arrived was Darwin city centre – which took about ten minutes – and the inside of our hostel.

Thankfully, we were able to leave Darwin that Wednesday, and we left it as we had found it; in lightning, thunder and torrential rain. After too many days cooped up in a hostel dorm drinking cheap beer and going slowly stir crazy, it felt good to be on the road again, with bikes that were freshly serviced and sporting new tyres, even though our constant diet of straight roads meant that the old ones were only worn in the middle. Still, maybe Triumph could sell them on to bikers who cornered a lot.

As for Matilda, she now boasted a new battery and alternator, but not, sadly, a header tank for the radiator, since the Wicked depot had failed to order a new one, then removed the old one completely.

'Listen, are you sure we don't need that?' I said as the mechanic threw it in the nearest bin.

'No worries, mate, she'll be all right. Just top the rad up every morning,' he said blithely. Only time would tell if he was right.

Matilda's bits were not the only new thing being sported, for in spite of my fastidious nightly handwashing, the Adelaide shirt I had worn for the first half of the trip had developed an ingrained layer of red dust, through which could dimly be glimpsed like palimpsests the death masks of every type of insect in Australia, and probably a few undiscovered species to boot; each of them bearing a fading imprint of the surprised expression which had been their last on earth, accompanied, no doubt, by the thought, 'Oh look, a Triumph! You don't see too many of those out h–'

Naturally, about ten minutes down the road, a grasshopper attempting to set a world high-jump record left its insides all over the outside of my shiny new shirt. Back at Bug Broadcasting, a commentator yelled into his microphone, 'And it's a gold medal for Gordon of Team Darwin! Whoops … better make that posthumous, folks.'

By nightfall we were back down the road to Katherine.

Since it was dark when we arrived we picked the first motel we came to – The Beagle. Glad as we were to get out of Darwin, it seemed like a sign. Paul was flaked out by the heat, so Geoff and I headed into town to rustle up some grub and beer.

There were a lot of Aboriginals, mainly men, wandering around in search of drink and we had to produce photo ID to get some beer in what must be a measure to try and minimise their drinking. The government and some of the tribal authorities have banned drinking on tribal lands, so it's only to be expected that those who want to drink will congregate in the towns, even though drinking in public is also banned there. They were a noisy bunch and probably meant no harm, but we were glad to get back to our room, have something to eat, do some work and go to bed.

Up early once more we were itching to put distance between us and Katherine which, apart from the beautiful gorge to the east, had little to recommend it. The gorge is worth seeing though and there are all sorts of cruises and guided walks you can take that will take you below the towering cliffs which narrow above you. The place is sacred to the Koorie people and it is easy to see why.

We headed west the next morning through a landscape which for hours was irrevocably, irrecoverably, irremediably and irredeemably, to paraphrase John Donne, flat.

The only relief from the unending plains was a particular strain of eucalyptus with a dark-grey bark and silvery green leaves, as exquisite as a Hokusai print, and, from time to time, creeks dotted with tiny pale-blue flowers, their banks blessed with bright-yellow shrubs for all the world like the whin bushes of my Tyrone youth.

Then, all of a sudden, red sandstone bluffs began fisting through the sunbaked earth, and before we knew it, we had dipped into the gorge of the Victoria River, winding through the dappled shade with the sun dancing cool blue on the river to our right and hot red on the cliffs to our left. We swooped around corners, like boys reborn.

The scenery and grandeur lifted our mood after the enforced captivity of Darwin and we each hummed tunes as we sped along. We felt like the whistling kites that circled above us as we swooped through the valleys, the road rising and falling as it cut its way around the mountains. Black and white cockatoos kept us company as we drove, with the only downside being the occasional smell of death as we passed yet another wildlife traffic victim. Even cattle aren't safe from the road trains, and we saw at least two cows by the side of the road, slowly putrifying in the heat.

Geoff even had a go at rounding up some cattle – at least that was what we thought he was doing, until he slammed on the brakes and we realised that he hadn't seen them on the road until quite late. It is surprising how well camouflaged they are, being mostly off-white with patches of black and brown. They stand under the trees and blend in quite well, looking like the myriad termite mounds, so after a while you just don't see them. They can also move pretty quickly and are in the road before you know it.

I came across one at speed, a slow-moving creature which had seemed to be going one way, but then got spooked and turned around and headed back the way it came – right into my path. I hit the horn and the brakes at the same time and it galloped off down the embankment.

Hit one on a bike, or even in a car, and you will be the one turned to mincemeat.

 'Song for the day?' said Paul as we stopped for a drink, he having taken over from Matt in more ways than one.

' "It's Me Again", by Melanie Safka,' I said.

'Never heard of it.'

'She did that one that goes, "I've got a brand-new pair of roller skates" as well.'

'Got you now,' said Paul, who then went on to score a major early victory in the Poggle Wars by driving Matilda, with her fuel tank a quarter full, past the Timber Creek filling station, then a huge sign saying in equally huge letters 'Last Services for 225km'.

We stood and watched him disappear into the distance, then had a slap-up meal of two pints of tepid water and a Magnum bar beside a pub and disco which was at full swing in spite of the fact that it was just gone noon and the thermometer registered 38°C. With little else to do, we had a look at the communal noticeboard on which one sheet of paper declared, 'Hi, I'm Meg's, Timber Creeks new rec and sports officer. Get in touch with me about my exciting plans for the Creek.' Meg's had presumably been sacked from her previous job as Head of Apostrophe's at a greengrocers.

Our next stop was at the WA border for a quarantine check, as no fresh fruit, vegetables or seeds are allowed into the state. A discovery, it later turned out, that Paul had already made when he was forced to hand over all of ours. But the inspectors Geoff and I encountered were polite and interested in our trip and welcomed us to Western Australia.

The state itself welcomed us a bit further on with a delightfully cool shower which felt like a spritzer from the gods after such a hot and dry day – we had a good feeling about WA. Driving into Kununurra was also a pleasant surprise, as Paul was waiting for us at the first garage we came to. Relieved that everyone was in one piece, we had a quick look around the town before heading back to the Kimberley Croc backpackers' lodge.

Geoff and I wasted no time and were soon making our way to the lodge's swimming pool, while Paul cranked up the air con in our dorm to max, set the ceiling fan spinning at a speed more suitable to a Spitfire's take-off velocity and collapsed onto his bunk.

'I think I've got heatstroke. I'm so hot I think my head's going to explode,' Paul had said by way of explanation, then slept all evening and all night. Mind you, he had left Ireland with six inches of snow on the ground, and arrived in Darwin in forty degrees of heat and 100 per cent humidity. I could tell it had been a shock to his system when he ran screaming back up the aeroplane steps and hammered on the door to get back in and go home.

Still, thank heavens we had had the foresight to keep two full jerry cans in the back of the van, or he would have ended up running out of fuel and wandering off into the desert slowly dying, like Peter Egerton Warburton, who explored this very part of the Kimberley region in 1873 with his son Richard.

Camels whose sores had to be emptied of maggots with a pint pot, festering scorpion bites, demented Afghani camel drivers and a plague of ants so bad that no one could lie down to rest either night or day were just some of the horrors they had to put up with. Not to mention camels so constipated that the Warburtons had to give them enemas using double-barrelled shotguns. Sadly, Peter does not record in his diaries whether the shotguns were loaded and fired, or simply used as conduits, but either way, it can hardly have been a pleasant experience for all concerned.

Slightly more entertaining, and a lot less troublesome, was the camel of 1930s explorer Michael Terry, given the sobriquet of Rocket for his habit of breaking wind first from the front, then from the rear, expelling the usual objects with a loud report and such force that they were a mortal danger to man or beast standing in front or behind.

While Paul slept off his heat exhaustion, I went for a dander around Kununurra before dark, passing at one point a group of Aboriginals sitting under a tree. By all accounts they do this a lot; having had their traditional aspirations taken away and, with nothing to replace them except benefits and booze, they are caught in a seemingly endless limbo between the Stone Age and the white man's dream of 2.54 children, a Labrador and a beaut ute.

'How you doing?' I said to one of the mob under the coolibah tree, an old man with a face which looked as if it had absorbed all the sadness in his life. He looked stunned, then his face split to reveal several teeth which were not on speaking terms.

'Doing all right, mate. No white fella's ever asked me that before,' he said.

'Really? Since when?'

'Since all my life, mate.'

The next day dawned glorious and true, with a sky so big there was no room for clouds. Paul, his head happily unexploded, leaped out of bed like a man reborn, and we sped west.

 We stopped off just outside town to inspect the 'mini Bungle Bungles' at The Hidden Valley, a national park which is a narrow defile with red cliffs rising vertically above your head. It is said to replicate the larger and more famous Bungle Bungle range to the north, giving you a taste of what they are like.

Sacred to the local indigenous people, the place was used for corroborees – dance festivals held to celebrate tribal victories or other events – and other rituals and so is administered by them, with the fee for entering the park going to the community.

The silence was amazing, with even softly spoken words echoing back from the sheer cliffs. It was easy to see why it would appeal as a meeting place.

Back on the road, we passed at one stage a sign for Lissadell, although it was hard to imagine a landscape less like Sligo than this, with its endless plains, eucalyptus stands and termite mounds stretching to distant sandstone bluffs. Not to mention imagining Yeats as a sunburnt stockman, keeping a cold eye on life, death and recalcitrant cattle as he languidly penned that Aussie classic 'The Billabong Isle of Innisfree'.

> I will arise and go now, mates, and go to Innisfree,
> And a beaut little dunny build there, of nails and galvo made
> Nine rows of stubbies will I have there, with a few snags and
>   prawns for the barbie,
> And live alone, mates, in the wombat-loud glade.

From time to time, too, we passed signs welcoming us to this shire or that; signs of a last lingering attachment to the old English ways which began to disappear from Australian life in the twentieth century after first the sacrifice of Gallipoli and the Western Front during the First World War; then the bodyline bowling scandal of the 1930s; the fall of Singapore in 1942 and the realisation that Churchill was much more interested in saving Europe from the Nazis than saving Australia from the Japanese; and the final straw of the 1971 Immigration Act, which for the first time since 1788 denied Australians free entry and equality in the UK, and incensed elderly servicemen who arrived at Heathrow and were forced to wait in the 'Others' queue while the Germans and Italians they had fought in the war waltzed in freely.

Two years later, the UK joined the Common Market, and all of this, step by cruel step, made Australians increasingly aware that their unconditional love for the Mother Country was not unconditionally reciprocated, and that they would be better served by turning to America – and in later years, ironically, Asia – as both friend and trading partner.

Indeed, the last great public flowering of that unconditional love for England may well have been the visit in 1934 to England of Robert Menzies, later Prime Minister but then Attorney-General, for the silver jubilee of King George V.

'The green and flowering things, a beauty no new country town in Victoria could ever possess,' wrote Menzies in his diary. 'Trafalgar Square and one of the Wren churches by starlight … young Englishmen with the usual attributes of cleanness, good manners, interest in Test matches and the championship at Wimbledon … we leave walking on air.'

For the rest of his life, Menzies was so devoted to the Royal Family and the Queen that even she was embarrassed, and today, the last vestiges of that ardent Anglophilia were only seen in the signs we were passing, for shires the size of Belgium, and for Downs called Alice, Margaret or Edith; sunbaked acres named by men soaked in red dust and sweat after cool English roses in floral dresses and summer hats, their pale skin smelling faintly of lavender.

'Song for the day?' said Paul when we stopped for a break at a dilapidated roadhouse.

'"God Only Knows" by The Beach Boys,' I said. 'I've got it at home on a double LP.'

'You mean vinyl? What a Luddite.'

'I am not. As a man who once spent most of his salary on black boxes out of Lyric Hi-Fi in Belfast, I can safely say that my Linn Sondek LP12 turntable still sounds more warm, real and three-dimensional than the hard, flat sound of even the finest CD player. Not to mention the fact that most solid state amps are still trying to mimic the breathy, ethereal sound of valve amps,' I said haughtily.

'I'll take your word for it,' he said, climbing back into Matilda, plugging in his iPod and driving off.

By nightfall we were in Hall's Creek, exactly halfway between nowhere and nowhere else. All too aware of this fact, the two motels in town were engaged in a battle to see who could rip off passers-by the most, so we checked into the campsite down the road instead.

Even then, we did not escape. The only place to get food was one of the hotels and the only place to get beer was the other, so one managed the remarkable feat of producing the most expensive and worst pizza in the world, and the other managed something similar with a six-pack of a liquid which looked and tasted vaguely like beer, but had no discernible effect whatsoever.

We finished both, felt suitably dissatisfied, and went to bed, there being nothing else to do; Paul in the van, Colin on the grass beside it and me on a picnic table. For the first two hours, we were kept awake by the band in the nearest of the two hotels, who played what sounded like the same song all night, then played it again as an encore.

For the next hour, we were then kept awake by the band's audience walking past the campsite. Sadly, they were obviously the members of the local Society for the Terminally Deaf on their big annual night out, since they were all shouting at each other about what a great night out they'd had. There then followed five minutes of blissful silence.

Until the rain started.

Gathering up our bedding, we decamped to shelter; Colin under the leaking awning outside the campsite reception, and me to a tiled slab under the corrugated iron covering the washroom. Only for every insomniac on the site to decide that the middle of the night was a really good time to do their laundry, wash their teeth or go to the loo, accompanied by much banging of doors and the motion-activated light going on every time they passed. You know, the one directly above my head.

At last, even they went to bed. Only for the Hall's Creek grasshopper team, obviously keen to make a bid for the national championships now that Gordon of Team Darwin was no more, to start their pre-dawn training session by leaping all over me. However, all was not lost. Realising that it had now stopped raining, I took up my bedding and walked back to the picnic table, and was finally falling asleep when it started raining again.

Picking everything up again, I returned to the slab in the washing area; only to find that now the wind had changed, and the rain was now coming in sideways. Thus the hours before dawn passed in a parody of sleep, as lightning danced on the horizon and thunder rent the sky.

 I had settled down under a tree, which was fine for a while until I was twice crapped on by bats, causing me to shift out into the open. Then the rain had started and it was relentless. Just when you thought it was slacking off, down it would come again, heavier than ever.

I lay there, gradually getting wetter and wetter, as the awning proved about as waterproof as a colander and listened to my radio which warned of 'widespread thunderstorms over the Kimberley region, with heavy rain and flooding expected in some areas'.

'Right bloody here,' I thought.

I had been listening to a local Aboriginal station until I twigged they were surreptitiously slipping in Christian records about every third song, without letting on, and so changed over to the ABC, where I learned all about what the current crop of Aussie actors were doing in Hollywood and how to make a will valid in every state in the Commonwealth.

I even sent my wife a text telling her of my predicament, but got no reply. I guessed she probably either didn't trust herself to answer or couldn't hit the right keys as she was laughing so much.

Just as I was slipping off, wet but warm, the heavens completely opened and water poured through every part of the roof. It was then that I remembered the laundry section in the toilet block which was open and I dashed over, only to find Geoff recumbent on the washing counter, looking like a blonde King Tut. As I entered, the sensor switched the neon lights on, blinding us both. It was now 4 a.m.

Mumbling apologies, I threw my wet mattress on the ground with a splat, lay on it, wrapped my feet in the wet sleeping bag and lay there waiting for the timer to turn the lights off.

At around 5.15 a.m., the lights snapped on again and I awoke to the glorious spectacle and olfactory treat of another camper emptying his chemical toilet into a drain three feet from my head. That was the last straw. I got up and stomped off, closely followed by Geoff, both of us in need of a proper sleep or, failing that, tea, coffee and sympathy.

Paul was also awake, having been lying in a pool of sweat as he gently steamed inside Matilda, unable to open the windows because of the biblical flood outside. When I went to pick up my motorcycle boots, which I had cunningly secreted under the eaves of the toilet block to keep them dry, I found that a green tree frog had taken up residence in one. As I shook them out to remove any nasties, he emerged and clung on using his sticky feet and looked at me accusingly – even the amphibians were trying to stay out of the rain. Losing patience, I told him to hop it and he did.

As restful nights go, it was down there with the one I spent one freezing December in a phone box near Carlisle on my way to a Leonard Cohen concert when I was a student.

'That was a ****ing night and a ****ing half, wasn't it? ****ing weather. Why is it ****ing raining?' said Colin in his usual cheery fashion.

I was just about to explain to him that it was raining because the moisture in warm air rises, then cools and condenses to form clouds and finally falls when the gravitational force down overcomes the convectional force up, but then I realised that being killed by a grumpy Australian drongo first thing in the morning was a sure way to ruin the day, and applied myself instead to the more practical problem of how to dry myself with a towel which was wetter than I was.

I fired up our little stove for coffee, and after making a mental note to suggest 'Hall's Creek – a great place to leave' as a slogan to the tourist board, we set off west under a clearing sky, the rising sun warming our bodies and our hearts and, far to the north, a ghostly rainbow lifting our spirits. Well, mine anyway. Once, two herons disturbed by our passing took off across a hollow flooded by the rain, their reflections perfect in the mirrored flat, and I finally felt that things might just go our way.

Until a little after noon, when Paul suddenly stopped and flung up the van's passenger seat to reveal smoke pouring from the engine compartment beneath.

'What's wrong?' we said, pulling alongside with our hearts in our mouths at what looked like yet another instalment in the Matilda saga.

'I, er, think I forgot to put back the cap when I topped up the oil this morning,' he said. Closer inspection revealed that he had, in fact, scored a second major victory in the Poggle Wars.

'Don't worry, chum. We're all a bit knackered today, and I did manage to leave the keys in my bike for two hours in Melbourne,' I said, as Colin cleverly jury-rigged a replacement using a bit of plastic, some tinfoil and a Coke can.

He may be a grumpy, endlessly negative bastard, but he has his uses sometimes. Or maybe I was just getting annoyed with him because of the stresses and strains of any expedition like this. As Sarah Murgatroyd wrote in *The Dig Tree*, her book on the Burke and Wills trek,

> Mentally, such journeys are just as testing as they are physically, and it is the small things that irritate ... sweat

stings, flies buzz, belts pinch, boots rub and water bottles jangle. Just the sound of someone humming a tune over and over or swishing a stick in the sand can be the final straw.

Even worse, halfway through the morning, I'd realised it was me humming the tune over and over again.

'Desperado' by The Eagles, since you ask.

 Hours later, and finally dry, we stopped for a break at a roadhouse in Doon Doon. While there I read a poster in the window which gave instructions on how to safely rescue a joey from its dead mother, whether kangaroo, wallaby, wombat or koala.

It advised that a joey can live for up to five days after the mother has been killed on the road, and instructed you to use a pair of scissors to cut into the pouch if rigor mortis prevented you from opening it. You then take the joey from the mother's teat, though if the joey is too young it will be fused to the teat, so you are advised to cut the teat off.

'Then wrap the joey in a towel or cloth to simulate the pouch and put that inside your shirt,' the poster read, 'This will provide warmth and your heartbeat will help to calm the joey. Then take it to the nearest wildlife centre, vet or police station.'

I resolved to stop the next time I saw a freshly dead animal and check out the pouch, something I should have been doing all along, but in my time away from Australia I had forgotten that it was the right thing to do.

Further along the road we came upon a cattle muster, something the tourist board had been trying to organise for us, but hadn't been able to do so far. The stockmen were using motorcycles, quads, horses, utes and even a helicopter to round up the cattle which numbered in the thousands and which created a cloud of dust that could be seen for miles.

I spotted a few that had managed to get onto the road and used my bike to drive them back into the path of the muster, eliciting a friendly wave of appreciation from all the stockmen.

Maybe I have an alternative career option as a jackaroo, I

thought to myself and, pleased with my short stint as a cowboy, I sped off after the others.

We stopped for the night in Derby, a former cattle town with a port at the end of the main street. The motel owner told us that 'in the old days' there used to be a thousand head of cattle going down the main street, coming from all over the Kimberley region before being shipped to Perth. But the town now survives on tourism and fishing, with people coming up from Perth to fish and get away from the southern winter, mild as it is.

The motel was a former backpackers' and it had a good kitchen so we were able to rustle up a 'home-cooked' meal, which tasted great after such a long while living on takeaways and meals out.

What bliss it was, after three hundred long miles on an hour of sleep between us, to have supper and a couple of beers, then climb into a warm, dry bed looking forward to falling asleep; a process which was hastened infinitely by the programme on TV, *Iron Chef*, in which four top Japanese chefs were pitted against four young hopefuls in a cooking contest.

The Japanese, of course, took the piss mercilessly, biting the heads off raw carrots then glaring balefully at the camera, and the two American commentators took it completely seriously, yelling to each other as the competitors sprinted up the steps to get started on the bell peppers on the podium.

'Wow, Bob, this sure is exciting!'

'Sure is, Jim! I think that's their fastest time ever up the steps to the vegetables!'

Sadly, I may have fallen asleep at this point, so I can't tell you who won.

The Boab prison tree

14

How our hearts lifted, at first to smell the salt tang in the air, then feel the cool breeze on our faces, and finally to see the glorious first glimpse of the sea, as joyous as it was when we were children on summer holidays, motoring to the coast with our parents in an ancient Ford laden with tomato sandwiches, flasks of hot water for making tea, screw top bottles of milk and sugar, swimming costumes, fishing nets, plastic buckets, spades and sandals which had not seen the light of day since the season before.

Yes, it was Sunday morning, the sun was shining, and we were boys out on our bikes for a spin to the sea in the shape of Broome. And with it the return of the slim and beautiful people. Australia, you see, keeps all the fat people in the middle, where it gives them more room to spread out.

Broome is on a narrow peninsula, so there is just one road in and out, but the town itself presents a pleasant face to the visitor on the way in, with buildings of corrugated iron painted in pastel colours, with wide verandahs and raised sidewalks. It's the centre of the pearling industry in Australia, some would say the world, producing the world's finest pearls using the giant *pinctada maximus* pearl oyster. It had a real laid-back feeling as everyone there is on 'Broome time' – as one local woman told us, 'Throw away your watch, you don't need it. The rest of the world will go on just the same.'

It was good advice and it summed up the attitude of the town.

Broome has a chequered past however, as we learned from our guide Glen when we paid a visit to the local Pearl Luggers museum. He told us about the activity known as 'blackbirding' wherein young, fit Aboriginal men were rounded up and put in chains before being marched across country to work as pearl divers or deck hands on the pearl luggers.

On the way down from Derby we had stopped to look at what is known as the 'Prison Boab' – a giant tree with a split in its side, which had probably been caused by a lightning strike. Boabs gradually hollow out with age, so a room, big enough to hold a dozen men, had been created inside the tree. The blackbirders used to use this tree to confine their prisoners overnight on their forced march, before taking them down to Broome and selling them.

This in turn led to another sordid practice as native men, sick of diving and its dangers, but still wanting money, instead sold their women and children to the pearl masters as divers. They proved to be the best of what became known as the 'bare pelt' divers, plunging to great depths on one breath of air. Pregnant women were especially valued, as the oestrogen in their bloodstream enabled them to dive even deeper and for longer.

Then, as the demand for pearls and pearl shell grew, the 'hard hat divers' arrived and industrial-scale harvesting took over.

By the late nineteenth century, Japanese divers had joined the throng, going much deeper than the native free divers in their newfangled diving suits with lead boots and brass helmets. It was dangerous work: dying to make money by descending and ascending as often as possible, one in five divers ended up simply dying in agony from the bends, and many more were left paralysed for life.

Nine hundred graves in the town's Japanese cemetery bear testimony to both the extent of that danger and to the scale of the operation, for by 1910, 85 per cent of the world's mother of pearl was leaving Broome destined for the buttons and cutlery handles of the well-to-do, while draped around the necks of the even-better-to-do were the rare silvery pearls unique to Broome, but found in only one shell in every five thousand.

 Back in the early 1920s friction between the Japanese and the Koepangers – natives from the island of Timor in Southeast Asia – escalated into all-out race riots, leaving many dead and threatening to overwhelm the local authorities, who only regained control after enlisting every white man in the area as special constables. The strain was too much for the police inspector who died of sunstroke soon after quelling the rioting.

But violence was a running theme in the industry, as the demand for pearls also led to black market trading as sailors stole pearls from their ships and sold them on. Our tour guide told us of one particular pearl that had earned a reputation as 'the black pearl', because so many people connected to it had died.

'The first was a young man who was offered it for sale and went to meet the people who were trying to sell it,' Glen told us. 'They knocked him on the head, but he fell into the river and they had to flee, leaving the money still in his pocket as he lay dead in the water. In the end, nine people were killed over that pearl until it was finally put on a boat and sent down to Perth. The ship it was on sank, taking everyone down with it and returning the pearl to the ocean.'

There were countless murders around that time, most related to the pearl and shell industry. It brought people from all over the world into Broome, and with them came opium dens, brothels, mah-jong palaces and every other kind of questionable activity you can think of. It was a really violent place where fortunes could be made or lost.

In a town of over four thousand souls – a quarter of them white and the rest Asian – 404 pearling luggers earned the modern equivalent of £33 million a year, creating such delicious decadence that the master pearlers, who wore white from the soles of their doeskin oxfords to the tips of their pith helmets, changed up to a dozen times a day in the sticky heat and sent their clothes to Singapore once a fortnight to be laundered.

It could never last, and after the Second World War, the rise of plastic was the death of mother of pearl. By 1960, the industry had collapsed, and Broome with it, only to be saved for the second time by the Japanese, who had begun cultivating pearls in 1926 and now returned to Broome to grow them where their predecessors had risked death collecting them wild.

Cultivating pearls is a fascinating process which involves stabbing an oyster's gonads. The oyster, understandably pissed off, produces a sticky nacre which eventually solidifies into a pearl. In this regard, its slightly disturbing origins are similar to ambergris, the substance regurgitated by sperm whales that is used in the making of perfume.

Which means that when women all over the world dress up and go out for the evening, they're wearing around their neck a string of angry oyster nuts, while behind their ear is a dab of whale barf. I just hope they appreciate how much we love them, in spite of all that.

Interestingly, we were told that the slime produced by snails is fairly similar to oyster nacre, so I formed a plan to round up all the little buggers in the back garden the minute I got home and make them work for a living. Apart from making me filthy rich in every sense, I'd never notice if they staged a go-slow.

Having sorted out my financial future, that evening I found myself in the town's Japanese graveyard, wandering among the shrines to the young Japanese divers who a century and more ago had come to seek fortune and found only death. And then I found myself, as the sun sank over the sea, at the very spot on the shore where to this day the Japanese community of Broome gather every 15 August for the ceremony of *O-Bon Matsuri*.

As geishas in exquisite silk kimonos sing and play the samisen, the men launch little boats which they have carved, loaded with gifts of fish, rice and flowers and lit by tiny pale blue lanterns, and let them float out on the tide to guide home the spirits of their ancestors who have died in the depths below.

I sat there for a long time as the sun kissed the ocean then fell to be at one with it, hearing in my head the infinite beauty of song and lute, and seeing in my mind's eye the pinpricks of quavering blue until they were finally lost even to imagined sight, and all was dark and still.

I walked back through the old European cemetery, where the seventy-six most unlucky Dutch people in the world were buried. Snatched from the jaws of the Japanese advance on Singapore in 1942, they had been sitting in Broome counting their lucky stars when they realised that the stars were in fact the lights of approaching Japanese bombers, which subsequently killed them all.

And then I looked at my watch, and realised two things. That I was spending too long in graveyards. And that it was time to go to the movies.

Carnarvon Street, where I found myself half an hour later, was once the home of the Japanese inns, brothels, opium dens and mah-jong parlours, but in 1916 it went downhill badly with the building of Sun Pictures, Broome's first cinema, to which the good citizens flocked every weekend to sit in deckchairs and gaze in wonder at the latest Buster Keaton or Harold Lloyd epic, accompanied by the spirited playing of the local piano teacher and interrupted frequently by announcements from the projectionists that there would be a short interval because the film reel had snapped again. Which gave everyone a chance to catch up with their neighbours on the latest gossip, since the seating was strictly regulated by race, with the best chairs in the centre reserved for European magistrates, doctors, sea captains, master pearlers and the like; the Japanese sitting behind them; and down the sides, peering around the palm trees to see the screen, assorted Malays, Filipinos and Koepangers.

In 1933 the talkies came, and patrons were requested from then on to leave their dogs at home, which both the patrons and their dogs naturally ignored. After all, didn't they have to put up with sitting ankle deep in water after the high tides regularly flooded the place while trying to enjoy Clark Gable sparring with Vivien Leigh?

During the Second World War the troops arrived, their tickets paying for a new projector, but in the eighties, the boom in video shops closed the cinema; until a good fairy arrived in the form of English businessman Lord Alistair McAlpine, who fell in love with Broome and single-handedly kicked off its reinvention, including a resort, a zoo and the restoration of Sun Pictures, making it the world's oldest open-air cinema still running.

There is something magical about seeing a movie outside under the night sky. As a teenager I used to go to drive-in movies on a regular basis and on warm nights would often sit outside the car. The audience seems to get more involved in the film at these types of shows, and often applaud, both during and after the film.

The film being shown, *Bran Nue Dae*, was set around Broome and features a largely Aboriginal cast. One of the scenes even features the Sun Pictures Garden, in a case of art imitating life. Paul, as a film-maker and general movie buff, was keen to watch it and it turned out to be an uplifting and joyous film, reflecting some of the newfound confidence and hope of the indigenous people now that many of the land rights issues have been settled and the government has apologised for the crimes of the past.

Next morning it was broom-broom out of Broome and back down the road, where we passed through Port Hedland – the town known as Australia's iron-ore gateway to the world – and a place called Sandfire, which was as hot and desolate as its name suggests.

We were now out of the Kimberley region and into the Pilbara, which was little more than mines and herds of cattle, as nothing much else survives. The hills are so rich in iron you can almost see the metal dripping from the rock under the relentless searing heat of the sun. Mining here is open cast – a process where they simply blow up the mountains, crush the rock, load it onto trains and road trains, dump it onto huge ore-carrying ships and then send it north where it feeds the ever-growing industrial maw of China. The other mining industry around here is for salt, and we could see the stark white mountains of it gleaming in the sun for miles around.

Highway One is known there as the Warlu Way, after the native people, and it skirts the edge of the Great Sandy Desert, a name which, in typical Aussie fashion, pretty much says it all – though even here recent good rain has made the desert bloom.

The Great Sandy butts up against the Little Sandy and Gibson deserts, just so you have a little variety in nomenclature if not in view. But the roads were now so flat that we could see the curvature of the earth as it appeared to rise away, just as the ocean does.

 The guidebook had described this stretch of the journey as 'world-class boredom through a dreary plain of Spinifex and Mulga'.

It wasn't wrong, and after six hours during which the only excitement was two corners, an eagle feasting on a dead kangaroo and a herd of at least a thousand cattle being mustered by three horsemen and a helicopter, we arrived at

Pardoo Roadhouse, which didn't even merit a mention in the guidebook, but which turned out to be perfect, with cosy Portakabins, friendly neighbours and even a pool where, as the sun went down, I languished with a beer below an elegant eucalyptus waving in the breeze and watched a squadron of white cockatoos practising their aerobatics. Dinner was a steak and kidney pie in a little restaurant with a waitress as witty as her T-shirt, which bore a cutlery set and the legend 'Spooning Can Lead to Forking'.

At the next table was Trev, a builder the size of a small planet with a beer in one hand and a fistful of opinions in the other, who was one of a gang of forty rebuilding a nearby Aboriginal housing estate which had been provided by the government.

'Bloody thing was only two months old, mate, but they'd ruined it. Silly buggers were even cooking prawns in the dishwashers,' he said, tucking into his lamb shank. 'Bloody boongs. Don't get me wrong. I know they've had bad times in the past, but say a mining company discovers ore, the boongs will say it's sacred ground and they need to deconsecrate it.

'So they do their bloody smoke dance, and then they say, "Right, it's not sacred any more. Now give us ten million bucks, and you can have it." I mean, if it was really sacred, they'd just tell the company to bugger off, wouldn't they?

'Course, it's bloody worth it for the company. There's so much bloody demand from China now that there are trains running constantly out of Port Hedland with 292 carriages loaded with ore. The first two cover all the costs of buying the land and mining, and the other 290 are pure profit.'

And having put the world to rights, he shook my hand – demolishing most of the small bones in my right hand as he did so – and went off for a good night's sleep before tackling another dishwasher filled with prawns.

Next morning, we were stopped at a level crossing by one of the trains he had been talking about, and he wasn't joking, I thought, as we waited an age and a half for the two-mile behemoth to trundle weightily past.

Port Hedland itself lay off to the right, an industrial sprawl of giant white mountains of salt, giant red mounds of ore, giant buildings which were presumably orehouses filled with dyslexic prostitutes, and somewhere in the middle of it all, the Pier Hotel, whose only claim to fame was that it once had the highest death rate of any pub in Australia.

As for the rest of the day, there was little to report, as we sped south through an unrelenting landscape of red sand and thorny Spinifex bushes, mitigated only by the occasional tree or corner, or by fantastical visions of mountains and lakes which rose shimmering from the horizon to seduce us, then vanished to mock us just as we had begun to imagine they were real.

By nightfall, after a long day in the saddle, we pulled in dusty and tired to Fortescue Roadhouse, the only place to stay for hundreds of miles; only to find that it wasn't, since all the cabins were taken. Luckily, the day before I had been reading the diaries of Ernest Giles, one of the unluckiest explorers going, after which I would have been glad of a razor blade to sleep on with a shoelace for a blanket.

Giles only decided to become an explorer after he was sacked from the Post Office in Victoria, and, undeterred by the disappointment of discovering Ayers Rock and rushing back to Melbourne with the news only to find that another explorer, William Christie Gosse, had discovered it a few days before him, set off in 1874 with his trusty assistant Gibson to explore the Great Sandy Desert, even though the name should have given him a hint that it was obviously a very large desert made of sand.

The two set off in good spirits with four live horses and a supply of smoked horse, which was presumably dead. Before long, though, they had set two of the horses loose, another had died, they had run out of food and were down to their last pint of water.

Sending Gibson off with the remaining horse to the nearest

waterhole, Giles walked on alone, and within days was reduced to crawling, his skin a mass of sores from the spinifex thorns and his head so light from hunger and thirst that he fainted every time he tried to stand. At last he lay down and prepared to die, but just as he was losing consciousness, he heard a faint squeak and looked down to see a baby wallaby that had fallen from its mother's pouch.

'It only weighed about two ounces, and was scarcely furnished yet with fur. The instant I saw it, like an eagle I pounced upon it and ate it, living, raw, dying – fur, skin, bones and all. The delicious taste of that creature I shall never forget,' he wrote later in his diaries.

Revived, he crawled on, found water a couple of days later, and eventually staggered into a camp at the nearest waterhole. As for Gibson, he was never seen again.

And as for us, we wandered back to Matilda and the bikes to make supper.

'Here, Dickhead,' I said cheerily to Colin as I hauled out our little gas stove, since we had taken to calling each other that catch-all Australian greeting to save the bother of remembering each other's names, 'whose turn is to cook tonight?'

'Mine, Dickhead. You know, it's very confusing us calling each other Dickhead, because we don't know which Dickhead we're referring to,' he said.

'Well, what about if I'm DI, you're DII and Paul's DIII?'

'Perfect solution,' said DII.

'Love it,' said DIII.

Shortly after, we tucked into our spag bol, Paul crawled into Matilda, since he had a paranoid fear of insects and refused to sleep outdoors, and Colin and I threw down our bedrolls on the grass beneath a handsome oak and fell asleep under the stars.

I woke a few times during the night to see, a few inches from my nose, an army of ants marching resolutely west towards the sea, watched by a family of bemused cockroaches. They were, I assumed, German ants on their way to stake an early claim to the beach with tiny towels, and I fell asleep again, to be woken at dawn by the luting call of a magpie perched on a branch above my head.

By nightfall we were in Exmouth, and had found a room with a kitchen attached.

'Fancy cooking tonight, DIII?' I said as we climbed off the bikes.

'I don't cook,' said Paul.

'You don't cook? What do you eat?'

'Ready meals. By the way, what was the song for today?' he asked in a clever attempt at a subject change.

'"The Air That I Breathe" by The Hollies,' I said.

'You're just a hopeless romantic, old bean,' said DII.

'Not at all. I'm a hopeful romantic,' I said, and went to the supermarket to buy some ingredients to wean Paul off TV dinners, then had an early night, since in the morning we had a little date with a big fish.

15

The whale shark is a shark the size of a whale.

At up to 60ft long and one hundred years old, it is both the biggest and the longest living fish in the sea, not to mention the thickest-skinned animal on the planet. Apart from the human male. And we were just about to meet one, courtesy of Paul and Lauren of Ocean Eco Adventures, who we found waiting in a boat by the beach for a tour group. When they arrived, all the men fell in love with Lauren, and just to keep things fair, all the women fell in love with Paul.

We climbed into the boat, donned wetsuit, snorkel and flippers, an outfit I was already familiar with from Saturday nights in the bedroom at home, and we motored out to sea while a spotter plane circled overhead. Suddenly the radio crackled into life with the news that the plane had seen a large shark to the west, and the boat surged forward under full throttle.

There was an almost palpable air of excitement on board as Paul throttled back at the exact moment that a large dorsal fin broke the surface fifty yards away.

'There she is. And she's a big one. Let's go,' said Lauren, and we slid into the water.

After about five minutes of frantic flippering, I thought I'd better stick my mask in the water and see what was happening.

I was greeted with the sight of the mammoth beast gracefully sashaying past only a few feet from my nose, covered in a multitude of white dots like disco lights which made it look like a fat girl auditioning for *Saturday Night Fever*.

It was an astonishing moment, followed by an astonishing afternoon in which most of the Indian Ocean, which had sneaked into my mask through my moustache, poured out of my nose.

This was the part of the trip I had been most looking forward to. Swimming with sharks was something I had wanted to do since I was about five years old, when I used to sit down with my family every Sunday night to watch *The Undersea World of Jacques Cousteau* and first saw footage of these gentle mammoths of the deep.

Ocean Eco Adventure prides itself on providing education as well as the thrill of swimming with these giants, and all the crew members are a mine of information, not just about the whale sharks, but the whole marine environment. So it was with considerable excitement that I sat through the company's safety briefings, which were only interrupted by Geoff's jokes about the emergency exits being everywhere. They told us about the strict rules that have been put in place for swimming with whale sharks – you should not get any closer than four metres to the shark and must always swim behind its pectoral fins. This was understandable considering that they have been classed as being at risk of extinction; while the sharks are protected in Australian waters, other countries still hunt them for their meat.

Lauren and Paul took us to Ningaloo Reef, which is just like the Great Barrier Reef, only lesser known and much more accessible. Closer to shore than the barrier reef – in places like Coral Bay further down the WA coast it lies just yards from the beach – Ningaloo is also a pretty reliable location from which to see the sharks as they frequent the area for a good part of the year. The theory is that they rise to the surface there for three reasons – to feed; because there is more oxygen created by the meeting of two ocean currents; and simply to bask in the sun, just as we do.

My first glimpse of a shark was just stunning. Despite all the TV documentaries I had watched I was still unprepared for the sheer size and bulk of the fish, which was a male of around five to six metres. The sharks are attracted by the bubbles that swimmers create, believing them to be food like small fish or krill and, as we were creating a bit of disturbance, it was not surprising that the shark decided to come and have a look. All too soon though, he dived and we lost sight of him, so the boat picked us up and we moved on. Elated and chattering like kids about our experience, we were more than ready to do it all again.

After lunch we picked up another slightly smaller shark, which turned out to be a young female. Like most youngsters of any species, she was much more playful and continually swam towards us as we tried to get out of the way, causing some mild panic among the less competent swimmers. After around an hour, she too decided it was time to go and disappeared into the deep.

I spent the rest of the day swimming with the sharks, taking every chance I could to get into the water. Having grown up practically living on the beach, I feel completely at home in the ocean, but after a final snorkel, when I got a chance to admire the rainbow colours of the reef fish as they flashed among the coral, it was time to go.

On the way back to shore, having survived the terrors of the deep, I was attacked by the terrors of a German woman determined to prove that everything they say about Germans is true.

'Ver are you going to next?' she demanded.

'Monkey Mia, to cavort with dolphins. It'll take us a couple of days to get there,' I said.

'I zink you will find it vill take you seven hours and nine

minutes. It is approximately 684 kilometres, and when I left there at 6.15 a.m. yesterday morning, I vas here at 1.24 p.m. Haf you been to Broome to see ze stairway to ze moon, when ze full moon is reflected on ze waves?'

'No, we –'

'It is not especially dramatic, compared to ze sound and light show at Petra. Haf you been to Jordan? It is my favourite country in ze vorld. Australia is my fifth favourite, followed by Switzerland, Argentina ...'

Sadly, I must haf nodded off at zis point, and was rescued by Lauren, who woke me to tell me that we had arrived back at the beach, and that I won the unsynchronised swimmer of the year award.

As days go, they don't get much better; not only for me, but for the whale shark, who by now was down at the fish bar saying to all his mates, 'Jeez, you'll never believe the size of the human I saw this morning, mate. Must have been at least 6ft 7in. Incredibly white legs. Fancy another beer to wash down that plankton?'

As you can imagine after a day like that, we slept the sleep of the blessed, then woke at dawn and rode south to say thanks to a bunch of unsung heroes without whom we wouldn't be here, never mind riding motorbikes.

Stromatolites. These are colonies of algae that for the past three billion years have been living in saline water, trapping sediment and producing the oxygen which eventually leads to more complex life forms like lawyers and accountants. Nevertheless, we should be grateful, for without them the earth would still consist of nothing but salty pools like that at Hamelin, where we stopped by to see them at work and catch a glimpse of just how things used to be. Pretty dull, that's how.

Anyway, fascinating as stromatolites were, they were not really the reason we were there, for, as I had told my German friend, we were on our way to a place called Monkey Mia in Shark Bay to give some dolphins their brekkie. You see, back in the sixties, when everyone, like, loved each other, the dolphins at Monkey Mia had started coming inshore and playing with bathers for no obvious reason.

Today, they're still at it, to the extent that pretty much everything we know about dolphins is based on the study of one extended family at Monkey Mia; which may seem to the statisticians among you to be the equivalent of visitors from another planet basing their conclusions about humanity on watching *The Simpsons*.

Still, the research has taught us that dolphins are one of the very few creatures to use tools, sticking a piece of sponge on their noses to stir up fish from the seabed, and that in other ways they're very much like us, with the women hanging out together and bringing up the kids, and the blokes spending their days fishing and chasing women. Er, except for one called Samu, a juvenile dolphin who's still hanging around with the gals, making him either a mummy's boy or the world's first gay dolphin.

They're also great timekeepers, for the next morning, they were there at 7.30 on the dot for their brekkie from the folks at the Monkey Mia Dolphin Resort, after which they buggered off to tell their mates, 'Yeah, the humans were there, regular as clockwork.'

There is, almost certainly, a *Rough Guide for Dolphins* which contains the entry, 'Monkey Mia. Free breakfasts from 7.30 a.m. on, from large colony of breeding humans who throw away perfectly good fish. Silly buggers.'

 There is a no-touch policy because of the risk of humans passing on disease, but onlookers are encouraged to feed the dolphins under supervision from marine park rangers and volunteers, with children getting priority. There is no real need to touch them anyway as they come right up to you in the shallows, making for some really wonderful photos.

After our frolick with the dolphins, we boarded the *Shotover* – a famous and record-breaking former racing catamaran – for a wildlife tour of Shark Bay, which was so named because it is home to a wide variety of sharks, including the infamous tiger shark. But the bay is also populated by turtles, rays, dolphins and dugongs.

Almost as soon as we had left shore we spotted some dolphins and then a big loggerhead turtle whom we had caught unawares and who drifted between the two pontoons and under the boat before he realised what was going on.

Then we went looking for dugongs. Also known as a sea cow, a dugong is a marine mammal which looks something like a cross between a walrus, small whale and a seal. They live on sea grass, eating around forty kilograms of the stuff a day and, as Shark Bay has the largest sea-grass banks in the world, it is home to around 10 per cent of the world's dugongs. They are notoriously shy animals and are usually quite hard to spot, but soon one of the crew spotted a male that they call Patches, due to the white mark on his back where he got sunburnt after being caught inshore by the tide. He is an old bloke and was very wary and expert at disappearing, but we did catch a glimpse of him, if only for just a second.

 Nine-feet long and ginger in colour, with a beard, nostrils on top of its head and a fat body ending in a tail which God obviously had left over from something much smaller, the dugong can consider itself lucky there are no mirrors in the ocean. It is always thought to be the inspiration behind sailors' tales of mermaids, which suggests that the sailors in question had been at the grog again.

As I was that evening. Feeling tired beyond measure at the endless days of riding, writing, blogging, filming, organising the day-to-day schedule for all three of us, sorting out personality clashes, shopping and cooking now that we were running increasingly low on funds and staying in hostels or camping, I was wandering past a local bar when I noticed they were doing bottles of Margaret River Red for a piffling $18.50, which was cheaper than three bottles of beer.

Bottle and takeaway hamburger from the same bar tucked

under my arm, I decamped to my room, sat on the balcony as the sun went down over the bay, tucked into my hamburger, had my first glass of wine of the entire trip and felt at peace for the first time in quite a while.

It was a feeling which lasted well into the next day, as we rode south through more endless nothingness. You could see why people were driven to drink to the extent that when the Western Australia government passed a law several years ago limiting Sunday drinking to five hours, the three pubs in nearby Carnarvon – the Port, the Gascoyne and the Carnarvon – came to a gentleman's agreement to stagger their rota to ensure fifteen hours of Sabbath boozing interrupted only by the short stagger between each one.

Hitting the main highway again though, it wasn't long before the scenery started to change. I noticed the red dust starting to give way to a more orange, sandy soil. The stunted Mulga and Ti tree were becoming greener, taller and generally thicker on the ground. It was still very arid, but to our eyes, accustomed to looking at nothing for weeks but red soil, rocks and grey scrub, it looked almost lush. We noticed great wheat paddocks, the first sign of arable cultivation since we left Queensland.

On top of this, the roads were fenced, so there was no more wandering stock trying to kill us. It was also getting much cooler and soon we were able to ride comfortably with our gear on, including our gloves, which we had not worn since NSW. We were out of the outback, now we were just in the bush.

By lunchtime we were passing Kalbarri, where in the 1920s a wandering stockman discovered the remains of a castaway's camp on the clifftops. Subsequent excavation at the base of the cliff revealed the wreckage of the three-hundred-year-old Dutch trader *Zuytdorp*, but no human remains; until DNA analysis of the local aborigines showed traces of the rare Ellis-van Creveld Syndrome, endemic in seventeenth-century Holland, proving that some sailors had survived the wreck and got on very well indeed with the natives. That, and the fact that the local Aborigines are all blond, seven-feet tall and smoke dope.

Leaving behind a solved mystery, we turned west for another one, bumping along a dirt track for one of the strangest places in Oz – the country's only independent monarchy and tax haven. This was the brainchild of Leonard George Casley, who in the fifties was a mathematician and physicist working with NASA, in between farming wheat in the rolling hills of Hutt River.

In 1969, he sent off his usual wheat production figures to the government saying that he had ten thousand acres ready to sell, and the government sent back the news that he was only allowed to sell 1,647. Naturally, Leonard did what any reasonable man would do: founded the Hutt River Principality as an independent state, refused to pay tax and declared himself as HRH Prince Leonard, his wife as Her Serene Highness Princess Shirley, and their eldest son as the heir apparent, Crown Prince Ian.

Amazingly, he got away with it. The government decided there was nothing they could do about him, and the principality stayed in place, with official languages of English, French and Esperanto, a population of twenty and a worldwide citizenship of thirteen thousand fans, a navy in spite of being entirely landlocked and an industry based on exporting wildflowers, coins and stamps.

After Australia Post refused to recognise the stamps in 1976, forcing Hutt River mail to be redirected via Canada, Prince Leonard declared war. Thankfully, Australia then backed down, avoiding carnage on a scale which can hardly be imagined.

Best of all, we were passing by on 21 April, the fortieth anniversary of the principality. After crossing the border in a cloud of red dust, we arrived to find Her Serene Highness Princess Shirley in residence at Government House, also known as serving behind the post office counter.

'Leonard's gone into Northampton with Ian to sort out some things for the weekend celebrations, but they should be back soon,' she said, and sure enough, the other two thirds of the Royal Family arrived shortly after in a ute.

Before long, we had been granted an exclusive interview with the eighty-four-year-old monarch, in which he expounded the history of mathematics, physics, jurisprudence, the principality and wheat farming at such length and in such detail that by the end we were entirely convinced that his royal family was just as loopy as we have come to expect from our own.

'You blokes staying for the weekend? We've got a brass band and a pipe band, a grand ceremony in the chapel involving several knightings, a nice family dinner, although everyone's welcome, and a visit by the Royal Enfield Club, since I'm president of that,' he said.

'Afraid not, unless there's any chance of being made a knight,' said Colin.

'Not at this stage, but log onto our website and you never know next time. Still, give us your passports and I'll stamp them to make up for your disappointment,' said the prince, sending us on our way with a regal wave.

Sadly, having been touched by royalty, we ended the day as commoners, in the gloomiest hostel yet; a rambling seafront mansion in Geraldton with bulbs which gave out the light of a jaundiced glow worm. Still, the discoveries of a cheap Thai takeaway next door, the remains of my bottle of red wine from the night before, and the fact that we were sharing the dorm with two cheery Israeli girls, almost made up for our disappointment at not being knighted earlier in the day.

In the morning, we set off for Perth in plummeting rain and matching temperatures.

We were heading down the Batavia Coast – named after a famous and tragic Dutch shipwreck back in 1629, where the survivors had turned on each other, resulting in a bloody massacre with 125 people murdered – and as we rode huge sand dunes appeared on our right, with million-dollar mansions perched up on the hills behind. Further out, there were some magnificent old homesteads built out of the local sandstone, which blended in with the landscape and looked completely part of the scene, a bit like the old whitewashed cottages in Ireland.

West Australians are known as 'sandgropers' by the other states and looking around it was easy to see why. This area had very little soil but an abundance of white sand and it seems the local plants have evolved to survive in it. Unfortunately the WA town of Eucla hadn't fared so well as, back in the nineteenth century, it had been completely swallowed up by the shifting sand, only to emerge every now and then, perfectly preserved, before being swallowed up again.

A sign from the local police kept me amused me for the next few miles. It informed passing drivers that the local fuzz were 'targeting fatigue' and I wondered how they went about doing that. If they saw your eyelids drooping, did they jump out of the bushes and offer you a coffee? Or a pillow and a blanket? Maybe they drive you back to the station and tuck you in and read you a bedtime story. The possibilities for positive public relations seemed endless.

Clearly I was in need of a break, so we stopped at a hamlet called Edeabba, where we spotted a sign at the local football oval reading 'Beware Falling Limbs.' I looked at Geoff and checked my own, but they all seemed to be well attached.

At the little café where we stopped for lunch, I looked at the rain pouring down outside and decided that the time had come to change from a Magnum bar to a pie as the midday treat.

'Careful with that,' said Colin as I prepared to bite into it. 'Remember what I said about the temperature.'

He was right. Although the outside was barely warm, even a tentative nibble produced a waft of air of a heat and velocity last seen when Vesuvius erupted. Even half an hour later, when I had finally finished it, the last mouthful still had to be juggled around, accompanied by vigorous hyperventilating, to stop it melting into my soft palate.

We rode on, and just as we reached Perth city limits, there was a thunderous rumble, and I looked up expecting to see lightning. Only to realise that the sound was coming from behind me; from Matilda, to be precise, whose exhaust had just disintegrated.

It was entirely my own fault, since just that morning I had been saying to Colin, 'Still, at least Matilda's going well, touch wood,' then tapped my head. So maybe there is something in there other than solid oak after all.

Thus it was that we spent the following morning as we had spent so many – in a Wicked garage watching a mechanic, in this case Paul from Edinburgh, toil away in the bowels of the van. That sorted, we set off for two of the three interviews we'd planned: top female drag racer Evelyn Scholz and stuntman Ray Baumann, who'd built a motorbike so immense he used it to crush cars.

Sadly, Evelyn was out of town and Ray had dismantled the monster motorbike so, sighing deeply, we set off to Fremantle on the outskirts of Perth to see Lezli-An Barrett, an old mate of mine from student days, when we'd spent a couple of thrilling summers canning vegetables on the night shift in a factory in Essex.

She'd gone on to write and direct *Business As Usual* with John Thaw, Cathy Tyson and Glenda Jackson, before Glenda's career went downhill badly and she got mixed up with a bad crowd at Westminster. I hadn't seen Lezli-An for at least twenty years, and lost touch with her after she emigrated to Oz, but a quick internet search revealed not only that she was living in Fremantle, but that her next movie was *Belly Dancing for Beginners*, based on the novel by Liz Byrski about a sixty-year-old pot-smoking belly-dancing Harley rider.

Even better, she had two spare rooms which we could crash

in, thus saving us the money for a night's accommodation. Naturally, to celebrate I then went out and spent the same amount on champagne and fish and chips, but as we sat tucking into them, with Paul chatting to her about film-making, Colin entertaining her thirteen-year-old daughter Miranda and me being adopted by the cat, we were all wallowing in the small domestic pleasures we had almost forgotten.

Incidentally, it was in Fremantle – or Freo, as the locals call it – that I first set foot on Australian soil, as our ship had stopped there as its first port of call. I had managed to get away from under the watchful eye of my mother and sneak ashore into the terminal where I spent the exorbitant sum of forty cents on a milkshake, the first I had ever drunk. I was so terrified of missing the ship, I downed it almost in one, giving myself the most incredible brain-freeze, and staggered back on board. Freo holds a very special place in my memories.

I'd never really seen the town itself back then, and being able to visit it as an adult was really incredible. So the next morning we explored the old town which had gone through a complete renaissance after Australia won the Americas Cup in 1983. The waters off Fremantle were chosen to host the next season four years later and the buzz around the defence gave the run-down port a big enough kick-start that it is now one of the most desirable places in WA to live.

It's still a big working port though and, depending on your point of view, huge cranes still either marr or decorate the skyline. It remains a popular destination for cruise ships from around the world and provides many people with their first taste of Down Under, just as it did me many years ago.

It's a great little place and it seemed to have an almost perfect climate – in the hot months of summer the breeze from the Indian Ocean, known as the Freemantle Doctor, arrives to cool things down, while in winter, such as it is, the climate is similar to a typical Irish summer.

I spent our last evening in Freo down at the Cogee jetty

watching the sun go down. Some of the locals were out fishing, and the pelicans hung around waiting for a free feed. It was very calming and it reminded me of my boyhood, growing up in similar surroundings in Melbourne. Of course, my thoughts then came to rest on my own family back home. I missed them terribly and wished they were with me to share all those magical moments that always seemed slightly tarnished by their absence.

The next morning, shopping for opals for my wife, I wandered through Fremantle and Perth, past couples and families sitting chatting and laughing at café tables in the sun, thinking how lucky the people here were to live in such a perpetual summer. No wonder they looked so happy and pleased with life.

And then, by complete coincidence, I realised I was standing in a street I had read about once, down which a young soldier called Len Hall had ridden in 1914, on his way to Gallipoli with the glamorous 10th Light Horse regiment. Seeing a pretty girl waving from the crowd, he had plucked the emu plume from his slouch hat and passed it down to her.

Five years later, having survived Gallipoli, being wounded on the charge into Beersheba and the ride into Damascus, he had returned and was marching in the victory parade through Perth when, as he reached the very spot on which I was standing now, the same pretty girl stepped from the crowd, touched his arm and said, 'Excuse me, sir, would you like your plume back?'

They married, and Len lived happily until he was a hundred and one.

I returned to Lezli-An's, opals in hand, and we left at lunchtime, riding south in glorious sunshine and equable warmth, bliss after the heat and humidity of the north, through gum trees lining cow meadows and vineyards, until at last – Colin and Paul having gone ahead – I found myself riding behind an immaculately restored pearl grey and indigo Jaguar.

As we fell together through the chiaroscuro of the late afternoon light through the trees, it was as if we slowly slipped back into a more elegant age, so that instead of riding a modern Triumph, I was astride a Vincent Rapide or Brough Superior, wearing a houndstooth jacket and soft-collared shirt, goggles and tweed cap reversed, on my way home to a little house in a grove for a supper of Lancashire hotpot and Spitfire ale with my wife.

But my wife was far away across the world, so when we arrived in Margaret River I had a takeaway pizza and a glass of wine, then fell asleep in a backpackers' dorm, my heart filled with melancholy.

The Margaret River Lodge, the backpacker hostel we were staying in, was a laid-back little place just outside the main town centre. However we had arrived on Anzac Day weekend, the anniversary of the landing in Gallipoli by the Australia and New Zealand Army Corps during the First World War, though the day is a tribute to the victims of all wars since. It's a public holiday in Australia and the place was full of young people who had come down from Perth to party – most of them were pretty drunk by the afternoon.

Despite a rather poor night's sleep, I woke early as Paul and I planned to attend the Anzac Day dawn service at the war memorial in town. When we arrived, there was a crowd numbering in the hundreds – remarkable in a place this size, but perhaps understandable given that Australian troops are once more engaged in a war far away.

The service itself is a very simple affair. There is a short statement about the origins and reasons for the service, then one old soldier will read out the 'Ode of Remembrance', finishing with the lines, 'At the going down of the sun and in the morning, we will remember them. Lest we forget,' as the flag is raised and then lowered to half-mast.

There is a period of silence, then 'Reveille' and 'The Last Post' are sounded. There is a short prayer while wreaths are laid and, after the national anthem, 'Advance Australia Fair', is played, people start to drift away alone with their own thoughts.

As the veterans and a lone naval officer stood in the growing light, some people could be seen quietly crying, either remembering lost loved ones, or, like me, just moved by the simplicity and dignity of the occasion. It felt like the most proper way to remember those who have served, fought and died in war. There was no triumphalism, just a simple sadness that anyone who attended could feel.

The service itself appears in varying forms all over the world, but it has its origins in Australia. It was started by an army padre who had witnessed the horrors of the western front. He had held a similar service for Australian troops aboard a convoy that sailed off from Albany just south of here, the last sight of Australia for so many of them.

When he came back he was coincidentally assigned to a parish there and decided to hold an annual dawn service to remember the servicemen who never came back. The tradition spread throughout the country and is now held in every town and city throughout Australia whose people gave their lives, showing the massive effect the First World War had on this country, as proportionately, Australia lost more people than any other country in the conflict.

I also learned from the service that it was an Australian reporter who came up with the idea of a period of silent contemplation at the service, which was championed by an Australian parliamentarian, and spread through the Commonwealth and, from there, throughout the world until a moment of silence became the traditional way to mark times of tragedy or loss.

The service is just the start of a big day for the older veterans as, just before the main parade, they go back to their Returned Services League club for what is known as a 'gunfire breakfast' – coffee with a shot of rum which recalls the 'breakfast' taken by many soldiers before facing battle.

They are granted a special licence to have a drink before

opening hours and to play 'Two-Up', a traditional game where two coins are placed on a flat stick, one heads up and one tails up. These are thrown into the air and bets are placed on the outcome. A simple but effective way to either win or lose a lot of money, hence its illegality the rest of the year. The veterans made us welcome and invited us for breakfast, but we declined, and headed back to our beds for a bit more sleep, only to find Geoff still snoring merrily away.

 I woke a few hours later, well rested and keen to get to our Sunday morning surfing lesson. At 10 a.m. precisely we found ourselves standing on a nearby beach with Jarrad Davies of the Margaret River Surf School.

Out to sea, several dudes and dudettes, all with matching Coppertone tans and six-packs, were catching tubes, or snorting rips, or whatever surfers do. I looked down at my own torso. In the days when I was an international volleyball player and could squat 200kg, do fifty-six press-ups in thirty seconds and three-hundred sit-ups without stopping, I had had a six-pack too, but these days the only six-pack I possessed was in the fridge.

Feeling like Canute trying in vain to stem the tide of middle age, I picked up my board and followed Jarrad into the waves. Jarrad was a former Australian champion and highly qualified coach who had the reputation of being able to turn even a complete idiot into a surfer in a couple of hours; after which I could change my name to Rip Tide, move out here and become, like, a full-time dude, man.

Sadly, Jarrad had never met such a complete idiot as me, and after three hours of intense tuition from him and several near-death experiences for me, he conceded that as a surfer, I made a damned good volleyball player. I shook his hand and thanked him for trying anyway.

 I, on the other hand, was convinced that I would finally get to show off my prowess at surfing. As it was I turned out to be crap – too unfit, fat and out of practice. My only consolation was that Geoff was even worse and managed to drink half the Indian Ocean for breakfast, which over the rest of the day, made its way back via his nose.

Still, it was wonderful to be back out on a board in warm water again, as the last time I was out was off County Donegal and the water was so cold I had to bring a hammer to crack the surface before I could get in.

As I practised I could feel my old skills coming back and managed to get up for a few short rides, but after what had felt like only twenty minutes, Jarrad informed us it was last-wave time – we had been in the water for hours.

An hour later and we were both at something I was much better at, possibly through years of dedicated practice: a wine tasting at the Voyager Estate, an idyll of Dutch-style buildings, rose gardens, mature trees, immaculate lawns and rolling vineyards run by billionaire businessman Michael Wright as a hobby.

After working my way through a Sauvignon Blanc, a Chenin Blanc, a Cabernet Sauvignon, a Merlot and a Shiraz, I was feeling much better about my surfing abilities and the world in general, thanks for asking.

The Margaret River is a popular destination for wine and food buffs as every business seems to be a winery, brewery, cheese factory or olive grove. Geoff was positively drooling as we pulled into the vineyard, feeling he had discovered his own personal nirvana.

As both of us were suffering from various muscle strains caused by our surfing exploits, we decided to taste everything, hoping that alcohol would work better than painkillers. Geoff decided to show off his pretentious side, spouting a variety of poncy wine terms and telling the vineyard manager, Britta, that he was thinking of buying 'a few bottles'.

'Here, drongo, which ones did you like?' he asked, 'I'm going to get a couple for dinner.'

'I think they might be a bit pricey, me old corkscrew, as she was talking about "lying them down" and all that, so if you do get some, you might want to take them home for a special occasion.

'Bugger that, life's too short.' And off he went.

I then heard the following exchange,

'Britta, me old grapevine, how much is it for the Sauvignon Blanc, the Shiraz and the Merlot?'

'The Sauvignon is $35, the Shiraz, $45 and the Merlot, $65.'

'Er, I'll just go and confer with my colleague to see what he prefers,' he said, visibly blanching, before going and hiding behind a very tall wine rack, looking like he needed 'lying down' himself.

Chuckling, I went back to my glossy magazine with its article, 'Wine for drongos who have no money and can't taste the difference anyway' – much more in my league.

We then snuck out while Britta's back was turned, the cowards that we are.

The next day, with time now on our hands after the long days in the Northern Territory and Western Australia, what bliss it was to wake late, have a leisurely breakfast and then gain all the time lost anyway by flinging the bikes around the curves of the road to Nannup, a sleepy hollow of wooden houses, a bowling green and a little café where we sat outside in the sun drinking organic hand-knitted free-range cappomochafrappuchinos and passing the time of day with locals walking their dogs or just themselves.

All around us, the trees were turning russet and gold, these being the early days of autumn, and from time to time the golden coinage of the season came tumbling down around us; ample payment for the endless days in the desert.

In the café window, a poster advertised a forthcoming concert by The Andrews Sisters, reliving Second World War hits such as 'Boogie Woogie Bugle Boy', 'Rum and Coca Cola', and 'I'll Be With You In Apple Blossom Time'.

And if that was too old-hat for you, there was a Beatles tribute band, a talk at the Wellness Club on leprosy or a jam session at The Old Church for 'singer's, songwriter's, musician's and dancer's'. Presumably organised by Meg's, who had left her job as Timber Creek's sports and rec officer for a thrilling new career sprinkling apostrophes like fairy dust all over the southwestern cape.

On the way out of town the next morning we decided to go and see the Bicentennial Tree right in the heart of the karri forests. It is a fire-lookout tree with a platform perched seventy-five metres above the ground, and from there rangers keep an eye out for smoke from bushfires and then direct firefighters to the outbreak. Depsite the modern practice of using aircraft to spot fires, the use of big trees is a less expensive and lower tech way to do the same job just as accurately.

The tree was pegged in 1988 as part of Australia's bicentennial celebrations – which marked the anniversary of European settlement – and the platform is reached by climbing a staircase made out of steel spikes driven into the trunk of the tree, with just some chicken wire acting as a balustrade and nothing beneath should you put a foot wrong.

Geoff and I eyed it warily.

'I'm not climbing that' he said bravely, 'I get vertigo when I stand up.'

I also demurred, pointing out that motorcycle boots were not designed for climbing trees, so it was left to Paul to rescue our reputation. We lost sight of him about halfway up, but he made it to the top and climbed into the hut on the platform, which weighs around two tonnes and which can move around four feet from side to side in the wind.

As we stood reading the warning notice posted at the bottom of the tree, which warned people that, when it was wet, the steel rods got slippery, and that climbing was more difficult in high winds, we found it quite amazing that anyone would want to take their life in their hands by climbing that monster. There was no ranger, no supervision, and nobody to hold your hand.

We were further humbled by the sight of a ten-year-old French girl and her mother scampering up the tree like Gallic monkeys, chattering away the whole time without a care in the world. So, after faking a picture of me around four metres above the ground, we took our wounded pride and slunk away.

Thanks to Dylan, a neighbour of Lezli-An who we'd met in Fremantle, we spent the evening and night with his parents in nearby Denmark. Rather appropriately, it was a hamlet.

Bob was from Baltimore, Marijke was Dutch, and they'd lived in Amsterdam, riding around on an ancient BMW with sidecar, then bought a VW camper van, done the hippy trail, arrived in Australia and never left, staying to found Wolery, a community of like-minded souls.

We ate lemon chicken and drank white wine, and talked late into the night about art and photography, politics and beekeeping. It was like being a student again, except both the wine and the conversation were more mature.

And then I went to bed in their spare room, a Fremantle tram they'd bought for $100 from a farmer then restored and lived in for six years while they built their house, an airy haven of warm mudbrick walls, cool jazz, recycled wood and minstrel galleries. I woke to find kangaroos lolloping around the lawn tucking into dewy grass; which was really no surprise, since the week before in Broome, I had emerged to find an emu admiring the bike.

We hugged Bob and Marijke goodbye, and that afternoon were wandering around the old whaling station down the coast on the shore of Frenchman's Bay – named, like Esperance and the Archipelago of the Recherche east of there, after the Frenchmen and their ships whose presence in the area in the late eighteenth and early nineteenth centuries forced the nervous British to hastily colonise the southwest in a bid to keep their hands on it.

One of those Frenchmen, funny enough, was the man who lost the arms of the Venus de Milo. When Jules Dumont D'Urville bought the statue from a Greek peasant in 1810, she was in full possession of the limbs in question, only for them to be snapped off in the ensuing tussle over ownership between French and Turkish soldiers.

Where they ended up remains a mystery, but D'Urville ended up in these parts six years later and went on to explore much of the southern hemisphere, only to perish in a train crash in Versailles in 1842.

As for the Albany station, it has gone from being a death camp for whales to a museum where you can follow the grim process of turning several hundred tons of live mammal with a heart the size of a car into several thousand dollars worth of blubber, oil, ivory, corsets, horsewhips, umbrella struts, animal feed and fertiliser. Not to mention the aforementioned well-known perfume, *Barf* for women. Because you're worth it.

It was so gruesome that I had to ride like the clappers to the nearest new-age shop, buy a CD of whales farting, and listen to it for an hour in a darkened room before I could face a beer. That's how bad it was.

Anyway, I needed the beer, for we had been pampered too long by the soft life of the southwest, and were just about to make up for it by tackling the last and most horrendous stretch of Australia yet: the Nullarbor Desert.

Colin plays the first ever round of Nullarbor boomerang golf

16

 The Nullarbor creeps up on you. From Albany through Esperance and on to Norseman, the landscape changes from forest and vine to woodland and scrub, then to wheat fields so vast that after five of them I stopped saying, 'Wow, that would make a good spot for a flying club.'

They are punctuated from time to time by farm entrances invariably marked by a pair of white tractor tyres or wagon wheels buried in the earth, below a sign saying 'Green Acres: Bob and Gayle Hunnicutt and Sons', or somesuch, and from time to time by circular salt flats glittering in the sun.

I got off the bike and walked out to the middle of one, marvelling that until eighty years ago this land had been a dust bowl covered in arid flats, until the government had rescued it from the dead, planting salt-friendly mulga trees to bind the soil, then gum, until at least it could be turned into wheat farms so productive that they not only supply all of Australia's daily bread, but keep Asia topped up with its daily noodle as well.

As we headed through yet more vast wheat fields broken by mallee and mulga scrub, I made sure to stop and take in the view. The last time I had passed this way was about thirty years previous, when the place was much drier and was still recovering from having been turned into a dust bowl back in the 1930s.

The clearing of the land and the use of European farming methods, along with some bad years of drought, had led to the topsoil being blown away and the salt rising to the surface. With the land so barren, people just picked up and left, heading across the desert to the less hostile east. Many never returned, adding to WA's population problems, and the government had to step in. The country's scientists suggested a radical change in the existing pattern of farming, advocating the planting of natural scrub in order to counter the effects of the salinisation and to stop the soil from blowing away.

Over the following decades, this led to an almost complete reversal of the situation. There are still salt pans and lakes, but they appear to have stopped spreading, and are now in themselves a tourist attraction.

They certainly attracted one particular traveller anyway – further along the road I spotted Geoff dragging his carcass across one and pleading, 'water, water' as he'd just walked fifty metres in the searing twenty-four degree heat.

Down a long road lined with plain trees which could have doubled for an avenue in Provence, we rolled into Norseman, named after the horse whose hoof turned up a nugget and sparked a gold rush. Before long, we were ensconced in the Railway Hotel, a magnificent art-deco gem which, at the height of the gold rush, would have charged a week's wages for a room.

Today, it was owned by a droll and charming Perth environmental scientist called Therese Wade, who had come out here to study the temperate forests, fallen in love with the building instead, bought it with her brother and was now painstakingly restoring it to its former glory with a heap of optimism and the help of a baffled Alsatian called Audrey.

Even better, it had become a magnet for adventurers, in the past month alone attracting two brothers walking across the country, and a microlight pilot who, in attempting to fly the same route, had come a cropper while trying to land on the salt flats.

We threw our bags in our rooms and went out to play golf for the afternoon on the world's longest course, the Nullarbor Links, dreamed up by local businessman Alf Caputo and stretching for eight hundred miles across the desert, with one hole at each participating town or roadhouse along the way.

'Be careful of your balls, gentlemen,' said Evelyn at the tourist office when we picked up our clubs. 'There's a crow at one of the holes, and a dingo at another, who keep running off with them.'

Colin, being an anarchist by nature, had decided to spurn clubs and use a boomerang with a golf ball gaffer-taped to it; only to regret his decision when his gimcrack device turned out to have a range of about thirty yards, as a result of which I thrashed him at the first hole by a resounding nine shots to fifteen. Still, at least we both beat the hole's par five by a healthy margin.

The next morning, we were filling up at the village petrol station when owner Mick Cassidy pointed to a postcard on the wall behind him of a naked woman sprinting across the road.

'The Nullarbor Nymph, lads. Keep your eyes peeled for her, for very few are lucky enough to see her,' he said in an accent which still had traces of London.

'Where are you from, Mick?' I said, handing over my credit card.

'Wembley. You know, where our lot always beat you lot at football. Came out here to help my brother run the local store, then had to close it fifteen years ago when the gold mine closed down. One hundred and fifty miners left with their families and houses, and that was the beginning of the end for Norseman. Oh, and I don't want to see you lads again today.'

'Why not?'

'Because I'm the local undertaker's assistant as well.'

Thankfully we had no need for Mick's services and arrived safely at a roadhouse in Balladonia, where we met Martin and Nick, two bikers from NSW. They had travelled this same route a while back and had decided to revisit the area by hiring a couple of bikes and doing a big figure of eight trip from Sydney to Perth and back. We compared notes, agreeing that it was no longer the tough journey it had been in the old days. The last time I had crossed and recrossed the Nullarbor on a return journey from Melbourne to Perth, I had remembered nothing much of any note, except the five hundred miles of jolting and jarring pot-holed track that was laughingly referred to as a road.

It was a long time ago and I was just a teenager, but my impression from back then was of searing heat, flies and nothing to look at. I remembered that feeling of dread at having to come back the same way. Then I caught myself on being an old timer and went and had a pie – it was home-made and delicious, and the footy on the telly made it taste all the better.

Balladonia had achieved brief global glory in 1979 when the space station *Skylab* broke up on re-entry and fell on it, after which President Jimmy Carter phoned the mayor to apologise and a brief industry sprang up overnight selling T-shirts saying 'I Survived *Skylab*'.

Today, the attractions of the town are even more down to earth. I had plenty of time to think about them, since they were listed on a series of signs by the road into town cunningly calculated to build the hysteria up to near danger levels: 'Swimming Pool'; 'Children's Playground'; 'Cappuccino'.

As if that wasn't enough excitement for one day, shortly afterwards was the start of a ninety-mile stretch, known for being the longest straight road in the world.

As we rode along it for mile after endless mile, I could not help but think that Zen Buddhists spend a lot of time meditating to find the nothingness at the centre of their being, which is traditionally an inch and a half above the centre of their navels. I've got news for you, chaps. You're wasting your time. The nothingness you seek is in the Nullarbor, which is full of the stuff.

But for those of you planning to travel this section of the highway, here is a list of attractions along the way, in alphabetical order and from west to east.

> A rock – it's a white one, about halfway along on the right. You can't miss it.

Surveyor Edmund Delisser, who named the Nullarbor in 1865 from *nullus arbor*, the Latin for no trees, got it just as right as his counterpart who named the Great Sandy Desert south of Broome.

After an hour and a half of this, we reached a corner and fell off, having forgotten how to turn. It seemed as good a time as any to stop for the night, at the clean and cheery roadhouse of Caiguna, where a sign on the door warned us to keep it closed, since all the snakes in the area were poisonous. And as if that weren't enough, all night long, an insomniac crow in the tree outside cawed with a dying fall, *Caw, caw, cawwwwwwww* …

All crows in Australia sound like this, the reason being that they are powered by clockwork, but only come with half a spring, God having run out of full sets when he was making them on the Friday afternoon of creation week, just before he lost his temper and made wasps.

The next morning as we rode along I noticed a strange phenomenon – various articles of attire hanging from dead trees. One was covered in hats, another in what were once T-shirts but were now just tattered rags, and yet another in, what appeared to be, women's underwear. Perhaps the tedium of the Nullarbor had proven to be too much for some travellers.

As we were once more on unfenced roads, we passed signs warning drivers to be on the lookout for camels, cattle, kangaroos and emus, but none appeared, which was a bit disappointing as we would have quite liked to see some camels.

Australia now has more wild camels than anywhere else in the world, the descendants of those released by or escaped from explorers and camel drivers working on the railroad and telegraph. Some are now sold back to the Middle East for racing as the ones here are thought to be the best quality in the world, having been toughened by years in the bush and virtually disease free.

All of a sudden we came upon the Madura Pass, where the flat plain suddenly drops away towards the Great Australian Bight, offering an astounding view of the plain from above. It looked just like the Serengeti, minus the herds of wildebeest. It was breathtaking.

At Madura Roadhouse the next day, the halfway point between Perth and Adelaide, we sat drinking coffee and looking down the hill at the Nullarbor stretching out to the horizon.

On the roadhouse sound system was 'The Power of Love', that old eighties power ballad which made women come over all funny at the end of discos and men glad they did.

'Here, who sang that?' I said.

'Jennifer Warnes,' said Colin.

'No, it can't be her. Although she did *Famous Blue Raincoat*, that great album of Leonard Cohen covers,' I said.

'Kate Bush,' said Paul.

'No, it doesn't sound like her either. Mind you, she did that lovely song, "Don't Give Up", with Peter Gabriel.'

'It's Whitney Houston, mates,' said the barman, coming out with our pies.

'Nah,' said the man at the next table, who was wearing a blue singlet, khaki shorts and Blundstone boots, and tucking into a chiko roll, an Oz invention which is like a spring roll on steroids. 'Whitney Houston did the original, but that version is by Celine Dion.'

'It bloody ain't, mates,' said a man who was filling up his ute with fuel. 'It's bloody Jennifer Rush. My wife has all her bloody stuff.'

'Here,' I said as we walked back to the bikes and van, 'that must have been the gayest conversation ever in Australia, outside Sydney.'

'Not really,' said Paul. 'If we'd been gay, we'd have known immediately who it was.'

Our reputation as manly adventurers thus intact, we rode east, and by nightfall were in Eucla. The original seaside town had been slowly buried by dunes so, around fifty years ago, the natives sighed deeply, gave up and moved a couple of miles up the hill. Today, only the telegraph station remains of the old town, its walls and arched doorways slowly drowning in the restless sands.

We stood there as the sun went down over the sea, then jolted back up the dirt road to our little room at the motel for supper and a beer from the icebox. Only to find that of the thirty bottles of Emu I had bought in Albany, there were only three left.

'Here, DII, what happened to all the bloody beer?' I said.

'Ah yes. I ran into the Korean drinking team in Esperance, and was trying to keep up. Did beat them at pool, though,' muttered Colin.

I threw him one, drank the other two, and went to bed, where I dreamt, not for the first time, that I was just about to do my A Levels and had somehow forgotten to do any revision.

 As I lay in bed that night, I reflected on how disappointing the Nullarbor had actually been thus far – it was nothing like it had been when I last passed through here. Back then it had looked like the surface of Mars, with nothing but arid desert and hardly a bush or tree, with rocks being the only thing to look at. The modern Nullarbor however is green, and the trees, though small, are plentiful, making for an easier trip with more to look at.

There are also many more roadhouses and fuel stops than there used to be which, while certainly convenient, lessened the sense of challenge and conquest. As a result, I couldn't help feeling a little cheated that this mighty desert was proving to be a bit of a doddle. Still, all things must change and it seems even the desert can be tamed.

I was now starting to think of the finish line in Adelaide. We were so close to the end of the trip and, after months of being on the road, it would be quite an adjustment going back to 'real life'. But I would have the satisfaction of knowing that we had conquered Highway One and had seen more of the country than most Australians see in their lifetime.

Certainly waking up these last few mornings of the adventure was a bittersweet feeling: on the one hand I was looking forward to going home, to sleeping in my own bed and having all the old familiar things around me, yet I knew that, as always, I would miss getting up every morning, putting all my stuff on a motorbike and riding off down the open road in the early morning sun, not having a clue what the day would bring.

As this morning proved, for we had been on the road a mere half an hour when we spotted three Royal Enfields parked by the side of the road, as Enfields often are. As I knew only too well, from having ridden one back to the UK from India where they are still made, the vagaries of old British bikes combined with Indian quality control created a machine on which even a trip to the shops was an adventure, although radical innovations such as electric start and a unit construction engine have more recently given them a disturbing reputation for reliability.

These ones turned out to be owned by Ian, Charles and Russell, who were making their way back from the Hutt River fortieth anniversary, having ridden all the way across the Nullarbor to get there. Naturally, since you can take the Enfield out of India but not India out of the Enfield, Charles had spent several days in Perth while most of his engine was rebuilt.

In a way, they were following in the honourable tradition of Winifred Wells, who in 1950 at the age of twenty-two rode an Enfield 350 all the way from Sydney to Perth and back on dirt roads at the height of summer, arrived back and announced that her machine hadn't missed a beat. She is still alive and well at the age of eighty-two.

How strange and wonderful it was, though, to watch them kick-start the bikes into life, to drink in the familiar heartbeat of the single cylinder engine, like the purr of a lion after eating a particularly satisfying wildebeest, and then to ride with them for the rest of the day, feeling for all the world as if I was back crossing the burning sands of Persia with Paddy Minne the world-famous Franco-Belgian motorcycle mechanic on two Enfields painted pillar-box red and lemon yellow, on my first motorcycle adventure twelve years before.

We finally saw our first wild dingoes when we made a stop for fuel – another box ticked in my wildlife checklist, though still no camels. This bunch weren't too wild though, as they were hanging around the roadhouse scrounging off travellers before disappearing into the low scrub without a trace.

The only truly wild dog, dingoes arrived in Australia with people from southeast Asia thousands of years ago. Once pets and hunting dogs, they have since made a return to the wild and are now considered pests by the sheep industry, due to their habit of attacking livestock. But I'm a dog lover so I'd always considered them a very attractive animal.

Back on the road we came at last to the western and treeless part of the Nullarbor. This was much more like I remembered it, though it was still unusually green, but I felt a little mollified that my memory hadn't been playing tricks on me.

At Nundroo, after a day of featureless plains, came the first signs of civilisation: wheat fields, little windmills pumping water from the soaks below, then farms and houses. Well, only one, to be honest, but you have to start somewhere.

Suddenly, late in the golden afternoon, we crested a rise to be smacked in the face by a cool sea breeze, and twenty minutes later had descended to the coast at Ceduna, the first town we had seen in the five days it had taken us to cross the Nullarbor.

Edward John Eyre, the first man to cross this desolate plain back in 1840 and 1841, had taken five months in a trek from east to west which saw the deaths of three of his party and left Eyre and his native tracker Wylie cresting a similar rise at the other side of the Nullarbor to see the little settlement of Albany, where they had long been given up for dead.

As they stood looking down at the houses of the town in howling wind and rain, Eyre wept as he looked back on the horrendous crossing, and wrote later in his diary,

> The contrast between the circumstances under which I had commenced and terminated my labours stood in strong relief before me.
>
> The gay and gallant cavalcade that accompanied me on my way at starting, the goodly array of horses and drays, with all their well-ordered appointments and equipment, were conjured up in all their circumstances of pride and pleasure; and I could not restrain a tear as I called to mind the … sad disasters that had broken up my party, and left myself and Wylie the two sole wanderers remaining at the close of an undertaking entered upon under such hopeful auspices.

Compared to Eyre, and even Winifred, our troubles had been paltry.

Ceduna was like a metropolis after the Nullarbor, even though it is just a small town. With many more people making the journey across the desert these days, the town has benefited from the influx of visitors. It also has a sizeable indigenous community, something we had not seen since the north west.

We booked into a caravan park and, after catching up on work and filing copy back to Belfast, headed out in search of food and beer. We found both just down the street and retired to our cabin to stuff ourselves with local snapper, shark and dim sims – a meat dumpling-style food with all the main food groups of fat, starch and cholesterol. Despite it being a popular snack in Australia, it was the first time Geoff had tried one and, since he came back for more, we could say that if he was not converted, he was at least not revolted.

We rose for the penultimate day of the Adelaide Adventure and for the the last hole of the Nullarbor Links golf course. After we had worked out that we'd both scored around three hundred over par, we declared the match a draw. My faithful boomerang would now be retired and proudly displayed at home as the conqueror of the longest golf course in the world.

We were now a matter of hours away from Adelaide, but before that there was an explorer I wanted to pay homage to – John Ainswsorth Horrocks, whose grave lies in Penwortham, a smattering of houses huddled around a church for comfort.

On the way there is Wirrulla, which was preceded for miles by signs saying 'Wirrulla: The Town With a Secret'.

'Here, what's Wirrulla's secret?' I said to a large and cheery woman emerging from the grocery store with a melon and a leg of pig.

'If I told you, it wouldn't be a secret, would it?' she grinned, getting into a dusty white ute and driving off.

We spent the night at the venerable Flinders Hotel in Port Agusta, and rode on the next morning, frozen solid by the rain and wind of the approaching winter. On our left rose the sullen lump of Mount Remarkable, presumably named with the same sense of irony with which redheads in Australia are invariably called Blue. Alongside the road, meanwhile, ran a pipeline which I naturally assumed was transporting pies from the great pie mines of central Australia, but which sadly turned out to contain only gas.

On the stroke of noon, we dismounted in Penwortham, walked up a grassy path past the little church, and found ourselves standing before the grave of Horrocks, who set forth from these parts in July 1846 to find good pastoral land.

From the very start, his expedition was prescient proof of W.C. Fields' later adage that you should never work with children or animals. Particularly animals: first the goats took great delight in leaping on the tent and eating it. Then Harry, a psychotic camel who was the first of his species to be used on an Australian expedition, tried to eat one of the goats, bit Garlick the tent-keeper, who was presumably wandering around redundant since he had no tent to keep, and chewed to bits the precious bags of flour.

As if that wasn't enough, one evening as Horrocks was unpacking, Harry lurched to one side and discharged Horrocks' gun, which was rather unfortunately pointing at Horrocks at the time. Harry was subsequently shot, although it took two bullets to kill him and he bit a stockman on the head before succumbing, Horrocks died of his wounds two weeks later, and 164 years later, we stood in mute homage before the plain grey cross and matching slab which marks the last resting place of the only explorer in history to be shot by his own camel.

I had half hoped that alongside it would be a grassy hump marking the spot where Harry had been buried, standing up next to his arch enemy, but it was not to be, so we got back on the bikes and rode the few miles into Clare, a pleasant little town in the heart of yet another of Australia's wine growing regions.

 Clare is right next to the Armagh valley settlement, so we felt right at home – it seemed fitting that we would spend our last day roaming around familiar place names.

Spotting an Irish tricolour flying at a small country pub, we decided to investigate and learned that the Irish had come here in force over the past two hundred years, and had become heavily involved in the wine business. The barman displayed one bottle from the vineyard of a local maker called James Barry.

'$270,' he said casually.

'What $2.70?' asked Geoff, clearly still reeling from his experience at the Voyager winery.

'No, $270, though you can get some for around $190.'

Geoff picked himself up off the floor while I put the bottle down very carefully, made our excuses and left.

We spent that night at a pub in the town, elated because we had achieved what we had set out to do, but deflated that this was the end of the trip – it had come so suddenly.

It had, I thought that evening as we sat down to bangers and mash washed down with pints of foaming ale, been the strangest of adventures.

My previous escapades – from Delhi to Belfast on an Enfield; Chicago to Los Angeles on a Harley; and Chile to Alaska on a Triumph – had all involved a destination, but this time the destination had been exactly where we had started. On the previous ones, too, I had written and filed a story and pictures every single day, whereas this time it had been a mere once a week to the *Mirror* and *Irish Times*.

But to replace that pressure had been the pressure of filming and blogging, on top of the myriad problems that come from embarking on a trip such as this, and from managing a much larger team.

Emotions certainly had run high on this journey. Like when Paul the cameraman had arrived for the second half of the trip and found it almost impossible to cope with the demands of filming and driving all day in intense heat and humidity, yet had gone on to overcome them in admirable fashion.

Or, indeed, when I had to cope with my own problems of being so far away from home for so long, struggling to keep my temper and patience at times.

'Song for the day?' said Paul as we all tootled off to bed.

'"Bridge Over Troubled Water" by Simon and Garfunkel,' I said.

'Soppy bugger,' he said, and fell asleep.

At lunchtime the next day, we finally rolled past the Adelaide city limits, and parked in exactly the same spot outside the same apartments we had left from. There was even the same girl on reception, to add to the surreal sense that it had all been a dream.

Except for the fact that all afternoon I wandered around with my mouth open at sights I had not seen for the past three months. Delicatessens! Day spas! Fashion shops! People wearing suits! Restaurants! And not just restaurants, but Thai, Mexican, Indian, Tibetan, Kashmiri and Nepalese ones.

For a simple chap who had been too long in the bush, it was all too much to take in. There was only one solution, and I knew exactly what it was. Down a side street away from the cappuccino strip, I found a branch of Target, the discount store. And there, reduced to $8, I found what I was looking for – the dark blue singlet that is the garment of choice for the traditional Australian outback male.

To complete the look, I should really have added an Akubra hat, tight khaki shorts and a pair of dusty Blundstones. But it is a wise man who knows where to draw the line, so clutching my purchase, I made my way to a little Italian restaurant on a corner, ordered some carbonara and a fine bottle of Margaret River red, and as the sun sank in the western sky on the final day of our grand circumnavigation of Oz, raised a glass to life, to love, and to the sense of adventure that keeps both alive.

 The Adelaide Adventure was over.

I had seen so much of that wonderful country of my youth, a country that I have a profound bond with, yet overall the thing I would take away from this journey was the ability to appreciate what I already have. Everyone should undertake a trip like this at least once in their life, so they can learn the same lesson, and stop worrying about the things they don't have, as they don't matter.

What does matter is the people around you, and so I was looking forward to being home and seeing my darling family. I couldn't wait to hold my wife and tell her how much I loved her, and to once again hear my baby girl say 'Daddy' just as she did on the morning I left. I knew that when I got home I would appreciate every minute with them and I hoped I would retain that feeling forever.

Thank you, Australia, I hope to see you again one day.

Onwards!

Glossary
(*aka* - Strine for Poms)

apples, she'll be – it'll be all right

Banana Bender – a person from Queensland
beaut – beautiful / great
billabong – river / watering hole
Black Stump – an imaginary point beyond which the country is
    considered remote or uncivilised
blue – a person with red hair

come the raw prawn – try to fool another person
Crow Eater – a person from South Australia

daks – trousers
dekko – take a look
drongo – stupid person
dunny – toilet

Esky – an Australian brand of cooler

fair dinkum – true, real, genuine

galvo – galvanised iron
gibber – a large rock or a desert
grog – liquor, beer

Mexican – a person from Victoria

Never Never – a term for the remoter parts of the Australian
outback

Pom – an English person
pootle – to roam / a short walk

ridgi-didge – original, genuine

salties – saltwater crocodiles
Sandgroper – a person from Western Australia
sheila – woman
shout – turn to buy (drinks usually) eg 'It's your shout'
snag – sausage
stubbie – beer bottle
swag – rolled-up bedding

tinny – can of beer

ute – utility vehicle

warm fuzzies – a feeling of affection, comfort and friendliness

yabber – talk (a lot)
yabby / yabbies – freshwater crayfish

Bibliography

BRYSON, Bill, *Down Under* (London: Doubleday, 2000)

CAREY, Peter, *Bliss* (London: Faber and Faber, 1981)

DALY, Margo, Anne Dehne, David Leffman and Chris Scott, *The Rough Guide to Australia* (London: Rough Guides, 2005)

DAY, David, *Claiming A Continent: A New History of Australia* (Sydney: HarperCollins, 1996)

FLANNERY, Tim (ed), *The Explorers: Stories of Discovery and Adventure from the Australian Frontier* (New York: Grove Press, 1998)

HABEGGER, Larry (ed), *Travelers' Tales: Australia* (San Francisco: Travelers' Tales, 2000)

HORNE, Donald, *The Lucky Country* (Sydney: Penguin, 1964)

HORWITZ, Tony, *One For The Road* (New York: Vintage, 1999)

HUGHES, Robert, *The Fatal Shore* (London: Vintage, 2003)

HYDE, Mike, *Twisting Throttle Australia* (Auckland: HarperCollins, 2007)

KENEALLY, Tom, *The Commonwealth of Thieves* (London: Vintage, 2007)

KENNEDY, Douglas, *The Dead Heart* (London: Little, Brown and Company, 1994)

KNIGHTLEY, Phillip, *Australia: A Biography of a Nation* (London: Vintage, 2001)

McHUGH, Evan, *Outback Pioneers* (Victoria: Penguin, 2008)

MURGATROYD, Sarah, *The Dig Tree* (London: Bloomsbury, 2002)

NIXON, Allan M., *Bush Aussies* (Victoria: Penguin, 2007)

SHUTE, Nevil, *A Town Like Alice* (London: Vintage Classics, 2007)

SMITH, Roff, *Cold Beer and Crocodiles: A Bicycle Journey Around Australia* (Washington: National Geographic, 2000)

STEVENSON, Andrew, *Beyond the Black Stump: Travels in Outback Australia* (London: Eye Books, 2003)

WHITTAKER, Mark, and Amy Willesee, *The Road to Mount Buggery: A Journey Through the Curiously Named Places of Australia* (Sydney: Macmillan, 2001)

Acknowledgements

We would like to take this opportunity to thank:

At Bluebird Media, Matt Curry, Gareth McGrillan and Paul McParland for managing to make two complete idiots look as if they knew what they were doing at least some of the time. A particular nod to Gareth for making the best coffee and ham and cheese sandwiches in the known universe, and to Paul for overcoming his fear of cooking to the extent that after two lessons, he bought Delia Smith's *Complete Cookery Course*.

Thanks also to Enda Murray and Alex Barry, Matt's people in Oz, for a sterling job in pre–trip research.

At Adelaide Insurance Services, specialist motorcycle insurers and main sponsors of the trip, Sam Geddis, the company's dynamic MD, and his head of marketing Nichola Pearce, who's almost as dynamic, but much better looking. And to Sam's wife Gloria for keeping Sam reasonably sane for the three weeks he was out with us. And probably the rest of the time as well.

Thanks also to Adelaide's insurance claims handler Plantec, a subsidiary sponsor along with the Institute of Advanced Motorists, whose instructors Paul and Lynn Sheldon painstakingly prepared us for our advanced motorcycling test, and whose examiner Charlie Stewart passed us, much to our surprise.

The Creative Industries Innovation Fund, which supported the project through funding from the Arts Council of Northern Ireland and the Department of Culture, Arts and Leisure (DCAL).

At Triumph, thanks once again to communications manager Andrea Friggi who, in spite of me throwing the last Tiger she lent me down a road in Colombia, very kindly provided not only two more for this trip, but a Sprint for Sam Geddis and our motorcycle clothing as well. The woman's generosity knows no bounds.

Also at Triumph, thanks to Mal Jarrett, their Australian importer, and the guys at the dealerships in Adelaide, Melbourne, Mount Isa and Darwin who kept us on the road.

At Wicked Campers, the incorrigible John Webb for supplying Matilda, our trusty and rusty back–up vehicle, who we shall never forget.

At Oxprod, Henry Rivers–Fletcher for providing three splendid Schuberth helmets.

At Etihad, the airline which got us to Oz and back, thanks to Louise Wheatley, Teresa Ita Lambe and Fiona Marie Lawless for their tolerance of our regular changes to the flight schedule.

The state tourist boards in Australia who helped us, namely Jovanka Ristich for South Australia, Lucy Pennington for Victoria, and the endlessly helpful Elen Thomas for Western Australia.

Gerry Millar, editor of the Northern Ireland edition of the *Mirror*, for having the wisdom, foresight and impeccable taste to run a double–page spread from the adventure every week. *Irish Times* motoring editor Michael McAleer for running a six-part series; and Colin Paterson of the IAM and Tim Oldham at *Advanced Driving Magazine* for running before and after features.

Gavin Livingston, for providing brilliant artwork yet again for the newspaper series and book cover.

Wendy Dunbar at Dunbar Designs for doing an inspired job, once again, on the look of the book.

At Blackstaff Press, MD Patsy Horton, head of marketing Sarah Bowers, editor Michelle Griffin for her endless patience in the struggle to make it seem like we knew what we were writing about and proofreader Julie Steenson.